# GO LONG!

# My Journey
## Beyond the Game
## and the Fame

Ballantine Books • New York

# GO LONG!

## JERRY RICE

### with Brian Curtis

Copyright © 2007 by Jerry Rice

All rights reserved.

Published in the United States by Ballantine Books, an imprint of
The Random House Publishing Group, a division of Random House, Inc., New York.

BALLANTINE and colophon are registered trademarks of Random House, Inc.

Foreword by Bill Walsh, copyright © Bill Walsh

ISBN 978-0-345-49611-9

LIBRARY OF CONGRESS CATALOGING-IN-PUBLICATION DATA

Rice, Jerry.
Go long! : my journey beyond the game and the fame / Jerry Rice with Brian Curtis.
    p.   cm.
ISBN-13: 978-0-345-49611-9 (hardcover)
ISBN-10: 0-345-49611-6
1. Rice, Jerry.   2. Football players—United States—Biography.   3. Dancing with the
stars (Television program)   I. Curtis, Brian, 1971–   II. Title.
GV939.R53A33 2007
796.332092—dc22
[B}                                                                      2006051660

Printed in the United States of America on acid-free paper

www.ballantinebooks.com

98765432

*Book design by Katie Shaw*

B
RICE

MAR 2 3 2007

*To my wife, Jackie; to my wonderful children, Jaqui,
Jerry Jr., and Jada; to my mom and dad and to my siblings;
and to the best coach I've ever known, Bill Walsh*

# FOREWORD
by Bill Walsh

I remember it like it was yesterday, though now it's been more than twenty years. It was the first day of the San Francisco 49ers mini-camp in June 1985, and most of our veterans and recent draft picks had gathered at our practice facility to begin preparing to defend our Super Bowl title, which we had won just five months earlier. It didn't take very long that first day of practice for players and coaches alike to stop and stare at the new kid on the block. A few even gave me an approving nod. A six-foot-two physical specimen, first-round draft pick Jerry Rice was so explosive at every step that I think we were all in shock. I knew right away that Jerry was destined for greatness. He was so unusual, so different in his style and movements, in the way he glided along the field and absorbed the ball on the move. I had never seen anything like it.

Of course, I had seen glimpses of his talent a few months earlier, which is why I helped orchestrate a draft-day trade with the New England Patriots to make sure the 49ers snagged Jerry. Years later, coaches and general managers would claim that they, too, saw the greatness but just weren't able to draft Jerry. When I first watched him on film before the draft, I was immediately taken in by his beautiful strides. It was almost laughable how good he was. I had been coaching a long time and knew the wide receiver position pretty well, and I saw enough on film to know he would be great. So when the receiver from Mississippi Valley State landed in 49ers mini-camp, we knew what he had. What we didn't know was just how far Jerry could take us.

Early in his 49ers career, Jerry struggled, dropping ball after ball. I remember a multiple-drop game in preseason against the Los Angeles Rams, when Jerry broke down at halftime and wept in the locker room but summoned the guts to go back out for the second half. He had never failed in football and felt that he had let himself—and the team—down. Weeks later he would face the Rams in the regular season and break all kinds of 49ers receiving records.

There are three Super Bowl titles, numerous NFL touchdown and receiving records, and an MVP trophy as well, but statistics don't reveal the true Jerry Rice. The young man who stayed after practice virtually every day to study the game, to get better; the "coach" on the sideline who could see the plays develop and help our younger players; the receiver who sprinted downfield on every play to help block for his teammates and who inspired his fellow receivers to do the same; the loyal husband who was devastated by a wife's illness and stayed by her side; the consummate professional who understood why he couldn't remain a 49er.

There are so many great flashback memories I have of clutch catches and performances. At the top is Super Bowl XXIII when

Jerry and Joe Montana took over in the last three minutes to win the title. Or an amazing seventy-yard touchdown catch against the New York Giants on the road in 1988, months after his fumble against the Giants had been costly for us in the playoffs.

I was fortunate enough to be a part of many championship teams and have had the pleasure to coach hundreds of top-level athletes, so I think I have pretty strong ground to stand on when I say that Jerry Rice was the best wide receiver ever and certainly among the greatest at any position. Ever. The way he made catches, turned little plays into touchdowns, and played with such agility and stamina was never before seen in the NFL. He set the standard for the wide receivers we see in today's game—big, strong, fast, and explosive. He showed brilliance, stamina, athleticism, and intelligence and was the ultimate team player. His ability to focus and thrive in the atmosphere of competition is unparalleled, perhaps closely followed by that of Tiger Woods and Michael Jordan.

As one of the key decision-makers in the San Francisco 49ers organization after I stepped down from coaching, I bore the difficult task of watching Jerry leave the only team he ever knew. Things were not good within the organization in the late 1990s and early 2000s, and Jerry could not stand losing. On numerous occasions, I recall him standing before his teammates and challenging them to perform at a higher level and, on one occasion, becoming so passionate that he had to be ushered into another room. *That's* Jerry Rice. So with losses mounting and the team facing a huge salary cap deficit, cuts in compensation had to be made and roster releases had to take place. We didn't expect, nor could we ask, the greatest player of all time to take a pay cut, though we knew that Jerry could still play and contribute. I even picked up the phone and called the Oakland Raiders to lobby on Jerry's behalf.

Jerry was simply a class act throughout his career. His work ethic has become legendary, as has his ability to handle adversity, whether it was the boos from 49ers fans early in his career or the devastating injuries he suffered along the way. Jerry has an ability to rise above. He seeks out the challenges in life and attacks them with full gusto. That's probably why, when I heard he would be on *Dancing with the Stars,* my first reaction was "Oh, no!" then, "If anyone can pull it off, it will be Jerry."

The Jerry Rice that I know never truly revealed himself to the public. I'm glad he has decided to share his journey with you, because we all should be able to know him and understand him. Reading these pages, some things shocked me, and I've known him for so long. I knew he was driven but never knew just how much impact his relationship with his father had on him.

Jerry and I had a unique and special relationship, our careers tied to each other after that draft-day move in 1985. We have a shared sense of humor, a common love for the game of football, an understanding that preparation is the key, and an appreciation for how we go about conducting ourselves. As a former receiver's coach, I could teach Jerry the intricacies of the position, and I've never had a player more willing and eager to listen. We've remained friends for two decades, and I am a better man for it.

He is compassionate, funny, humble, and a loving husband and father, and he stands out as a true role model for all of us.

BILL WALSH
San Francisco, California
December 2006

# PREFACE

In the middle of April 2006, I boarded a flight in San Francisco en route to Hartford, Connecticut, with a connection in Chicago. I was flying across the country for a meeting with ESPN executives in the tiny town of Bristol, Connecticut, for which the closest airport is in Hartford, about forty-five minutes from Bristol. Now, as you might imagine, I have been on thousands of airplane flights in my life. And, yes, typically a San Francisco 49ers fan will come up and ask me for an autograph or for a picture, which I am quite grateful to give.

After landing in Chicago, I walked to my gate to await boarding the flight into Hartford. Slowly, people started crowding around, lining up for pictures, chitchat, and autographs. But these weren't middle-aged 49ers fans wearing Joe Montana jerseys wanting to reminisce about the 1989 Super Bowl. No, these were elderly gentlemen with silver hair, very young women surely too young to remember my football days, nervous little kids and their "soccer moms," most of whom didn't know me from football; they knew me from the ABC television show *Dancing with the Stars* on which I was a contestant in season two. Weeks earlier, when I had been in the San Francisco airport waiting for a flight to Las Vegas on a business trip, I was cornered near a juice stand in the airport and signed autographs for close to two hours, for young and old, men and women.

"I watched the show and really enjoyed your effort," commented one man, while posing for a picture with me. It was just one of many gracious compliments I received that day in the Chicago airport. In Hartford, ESPN had sent a car service to pick me up and take me to Bristol. Once I settled into the backseat, my attention turned to the driver, whose eyes kept looking at me in the rearview mirror. "You can dance!" he said in a thick African accent. "We all watch the show." I thought to myself that if a limo driver born in Africa living now in Connecticut was a fan of *Dancing with the Stars,* then it was bigger than I thought.

A few weeks before my Connecticut trip, while walking the streets of New York City, I was approached on the streets by fans of *Dancing with the Stars,* all wanting to talk about an episode, or my partner, or the final voting. And a few weeks before *that,* my family and I were in Orlando, Florida, at Disney World where I ran into future NBA Hall of Famer Karl Malone and his family. Here was an elite athlete, one of the more macho guys in sports, a six-foot-nine-inch power forward, who took the time to tell me his whole family watched the show and that I had done a great job.

People all around America seem to have connected with *Dancing with the Stars* and with the effort that my partner and I put in.

It was a refrain I heard often in my travels: if an NFL star is willing to try something new, to open himself up to criticism, to get out of his comfort zone, then maybe I can do the same thing.

Some of you reading this book know me from my days in football. Some know me from dancing on television. Regardless, the story and messages in the following pages are for everyone. It was only when I came to a crossroads in my life, completely shifting gears away from the only thing I knew, that I learned about the human psyche and how our potentials are limited by comfort zones that we all find ourselves in. It is so easy to give in to fear and miss out on the multitude of wonderful things in life that we are afraid to try.

Last spring, I walked the streets of New York City and stood in awe of the Empire State Building and the crowds on the city sidewalks. Believe it or not, I had never really walked around New York City. Any time we played in New York I was at the team hotel or the stadium. As I marveled at the vastness of the Big Apple, it hit me just how much I might have missed in life and I wasn't going to miss things anymore.

This is the story of how I got to where I am today and some of the great lessons I've learned along the way. For you football fans, there is plenty of pigskin in the pages that follow—never-before-written details of why I chose such a small college; what my time with the San Francisco 49ers was like; my relationships; the Super Bowls; what I think about Joe Montana and Steve Young; my opinions about Deion Sanders and Terrell Owens; why I moved on to the Oakland Raiders, and so much more. But there are also behind-the-scenes stories of *Dancing with the Stars*—what really went on before the cameras rolled, and why I made the decision to participate. Life is made up of memorable moments—some good, some bad—and I'm not shy about sharing those memories with you: The calloused hands from helping my father lay brick in the hundred-degree heat of Mississippi; the subtle racism all around me growing up; listening as my name got called on NFL Draft Day; watching the birth of my three children and the near-death complications experienced by my beloved wife, Jackie; the too-soon death of my father, and the triumph of *Dancing with the Stars*.

*Go Long!* is about going that extra mile, taking a step away from safe shores to experience all that life has to offer. It took me many years to learn how to suck the marrow out of life and recognize what was driving me on the inside. Maximizing that drive is the key to success for me, and could be for you as well.

I hope that you enjoy reading about my journey as much as I did living it, but more importantly, I hope you are enjoying your own journey.


JERRY RICE
San Francisco, California
December 2006

# CONTENTS

# CONTENTS

# GO LONG!

# Way Down South

MOST OF THE TIME, I'd run late in the afternoon. The temperature would still be over one hundred in the summertime despite the sleepy sun. Wearing my one pair of sneakers and a ragged shirt and shorts, I'd grab a small towel from my mother before heading out. Out the front door and into the country. The roads were dirt-covered, as there was no pavement where we lived. I'd run and kick dirt off my heels as I passed our neighbors' houses and waved to passersby. Being in the sticks of Mississippi meant "neighbors" could be miles apart. As cars passed me, the tires spewed up dirt all over my face and clothes as I made my way around the seven-mile or so circular journey. With sweat running profusely down my face, the towel came in handy, but in the last mile or so, when my body was aching, I'd often throw it to the side. When I returned home to our house in the country, life—as I knew it—picked up again.

Close your eyes and imagine a small town in the Deep South. A certain picture probably pops up: dirt roads, pickup trucks, hot sweaty August days. Whether you have visited the area, or simply recall a small southern town from a movie, your image is probably close to reality. Now picture that same small town *much, much* smaller. That's the best way to introduce my hometown of Crawford, Mississippi. There are no stoplights, very few street signs, a few broken-down sidewalks, and not that many people—somewhere between five hundred and a thousand back when I was growing up. But not only were we small in numbers, it seemed like we were all distant cousins. Everyone knew everyone else, and everyone old enough to be a parent was a parent to all the kids. You couldn't get away with much.

I was the sixth of eight kids born to Joe and Eddie B. Rice, two native Mississippians. There were my older siblings, Eddie Dean, Joe, Tom, Jimmy, and James, and my younger ones, Loistine and Zebedee. We were a big family, but close. I shared a bedroom with three of my brothers, so sometimes we were *too* close! We lived on seven acres in a house that my father built with his own hands, about thirty minutes outside of the "town" of Crawford. So you can imagine just how far out we lived. There was thigh-high brush, swampland, wild horses, and dirt roads, not to mention the nearly triple-digit weather most days. We had a few neighbors "within calling distance," as my mother would say, including my grandparents. I was a true southern boy from the sticks.

My father, Joe, stood six feet, and weighed maybe 280 pounds. He was the provider for the family and the rule-maker, and oh, how we all followed the rules. My father was intimidating and could be mean—very mean—but in the way he thought was right. Life was hard and he believed it was his job to prepare us for it. His intimidating scowl and raised voice would scare a common man, let alone a group of children. Occasionally, I saw a different side to my dad, a side that rarely raised its head. He loved to fish, and I would tag along on the hour-long walk to a nearby lake where he would stake his spot and search for catfish. He was relaxed on the lake and took joy in snaring a big one. But he didn't fish that often, which meant most of the time, my "other" dad was in control.

His hands were crusty from so many days out in the Mississippi sun building homes, laying bricks, brick by brick, day after day, all year long; sometimes he'd work two or three different jobs to get money.

In the South close to thirty years ago, affection wasn't shown much between parents and children, or even between parents. When it was time to be tough, my father could be tough. If one of us did something wrong, my father would instruct us to go into the backyard and pick a stick—a stick he would then use to beat us on our behinds and back, to teach us a lesson or two. Sometimes he pulled out a large leather belt and whipped us good. The extension cord hurt as well. He would whip me and my brothers *and* my sisters—no one was immune. The beatings hurt so bad that they were a good deterrent to keep us all out of trouble. I remember one evening, when I was about fourteen years old, a few of my brothers and sisters and I snuck out of the house to go to a neighbor's to watch the Jackson Five perform on television. We didn't have a TV but we were big Jackson Five fans. So, despite my father's insistence that we not leave the house, we did. The beatings upon our return left a mark—literally and figuratively. But that's how they did it where and when I grew up. I guess the fear of getting hit by the stick and the intimidating look on my father's face kept pushing me to do the right thing. And it still does.

My mother, Eddie B., was short, a conservative woman with a grand heart who welcomed any and all into our home for lavishly cooked meals. She raised us while my father worked. But despite the economic struggles, I think it's safe to say that my parents did a pretty good job raising all of us, treating us all as equals. On Sundays we would go to the Pinegrove Missionary Baptist Church for services as a family and in the evenings we would sit around the dinner table together. That's just what we did.

My childhood was like that of many young boys—I played sandlot football into the night, read *Sports Illustrated* under the covers, and bellyached when it was time to get up and go to school. In the summertime and over the holidays, I worked with my father laying bricks for homes and businesses. Bricklaying is demanding, tough work. We would be up at five a.m. and work until sundown. My brothers and I would be the supply chain for my father, who actually laid the brick and mortar onto the structure. It was our job to make sure that the bricks were ready to be laid down and the mortar prepared to be spread. On many occasions, I was the last link between the bricks and my father. My brothers and I would bring the bricks to a worksite and pass them from one to another until handing them to my dad for placing. Often, when my father had moved on to the second floor of a structure, I would balance myself on the scaffolding two stories up and catch bricks that my brothers would throw to me from the ground. (Some like to say that's where my great catching hands for football came from—I'm not so sure. Brick-catching requires hard hands and an aggressive approach; catching a football requires soft hands to cradle. Regardless, the hand-eye coordination had to help me down the road.)

Bricklaying wasn't fun work, but it earned us money, some of which I turned over to my parents to help pay for clothes and groceries. I do remember how anxious I was to make sure there was always a brick and mortar for my father. I didn't want to let him down. Time is money in the bricklaying business, so any slowdown in supply cost my father money. That's a lot of pressure on a teenager. I was afraid to fail. But you know what? Fear of failure isn't always a bad thing. It helped keep me focused on the task. And a fear of failure has carried me through my life.

It's probably a big surprise to many of you that I am so insecure about success. In fact, it took me years to admit that fear is at the root of my performance. It goes against much of what the literature and "gurus" out there insist, that you have to let go of your fear to ever be successful; that you can't be afraid to fail. I don't think that's an absolute. My fear of failing as a child carried over onto the football field in high school and then college. I was so concerned about not being successful that it pushed me to be successful. All of those extra hours in the gym or on the track or on the practice fields were more than just about hard work; they were about avoiding failure. Before every game of my NFL career I was scared—scared to drop the big pass, scared I'd let my teammates down. And now I realize it all goes back to not wanting to disappoint my father.

My parents' parenting proved that hard work and shared responsibility works. There were no slackers among us, as everyone had to pull their weight. Mom and Dad taught us that money is not everything. Mom insisted that love was the only thing we all needed. We went without on many occasions, meaning we didn't have many pairs of pants or shoes. Even a hearty meal at dinnertime was a luxury on many nights.

There were other ways to make money besides bricklaying when

I was growing up in Mississippi, and one of those jobs may surprise you. A big revenue stream for business owners down south was agriculture, particularly cotton and corn. To get the goods to the market, the products first had to be picked from the ground. I know what you're thinking: Isn't picking cotton something slaves did? Yes. But I didn't think of it that way. I saw it as a way to buy groceries for my family and some clothes for myself. My siblings worked alongside me in humid heat, picking the corn stalks, baling hay, and yes, picking cotton. I was certainly aware that many blacks in the south had been forced to pick cotton for centuries but that didn't stop me from earning a day's wage. Some of our black friends and neighbors refused to work in the fields and questioned why we were willing to. But to me, it was about earning money, and since we were being paid, I never thought of it as trampling on the memory of our forefathers and mothers and I still don't.

Sure, there was racism in Mississippi. We're talking about the 1960s and 1970s, a time when the civil rights movement was under way but slow to reach parts of America. Yet growing up, I never once experienced racism firsthand. No one called me the N word, no one painted racist slogans on our home or burned a cross on our lawn; we were lucky. But from what family and friends told me, I also knew I probably would get dirty stares if I walked into certain parts of the county that were predominantly white. Maybe it was because of my skin color, maybe because I couldn't afford many of the goods on store shelves in those areas. I did have a few white friends, a few white classmates, but for the most part, blacks surrounded me. There was an area down Route 12 we called the Crossroads, where blacks and whites hung out, but never together, and I did go down there on occasion, but always stayed with the blacks. (Years later, after I made it in the NFL, the whites didn't give me nasty stares when I hung out in "their" area, probably because I wasn't just some black guy from the country.)

One of the more unusual aspects of living out in the country lands of Mississippi was the thrilling and exhausting practice of riding wild horses. But this isn't a *Seabiscuit* story where you would wake up early morning, walk out to the stable, pat your horse down, and hop on for a dawn ride. No, just getting on the horse was a challenge. You see, the horses ran wild over the countryside, so if you wanted to go for a quick jaunt on top of the animal, you first had to chase it down. And that takes a lot of work and patience. On a good day, it would take me forty-five minutes to an hour to chase down a horse. With no fences and no boundaries, just imagine the size of the pasture we were dealing with. (And when I went riding with friends, we had to chase down the first horse, tie him up or use him to chase down the others, before we actually got to have fun riding!)

My favorite horse I called Pete. Boy, was he fast. He could make quick turns (like a good wide receiver) and his black mane made him easily identifiable. As time went on, I got faster chasing down Pete and the other horses. You would be amazed at what experience teaches you. I realized that it wasn't about being in the spot the horse was; it was about being in the spot the horse was going to be. I began to think one step ahead and it actually slowed down the chase for me.

I loved to play sandlot football or shoot hoops outside on the farm but I was never in love with any one sport and certainly never thought one would be part of my destiny. I remember Fourth of July cookouts and baseball games and I remember the Christmas days when I was given a new football. I never asked for one, I just got them. I'd go outside and toss the ball around with my brothers, but never put much thought into playing the game for real. I did read about and watch guys like the Dallas Cowboys' Drew Pearson and the Pittsburgh Steelers' Lynn Swann. I appreciated how they dominated the game—but I never wanted to *be them*. I watched our high school team play and was impressed by our quarterback, little man Kent Thomas, who was just five foot eight, but who took command of the huddle and the field, wore his uniform crisp and clean, and earned the respect of his teammates.

My older brothers were my playmates and teammates in our mock games of football or basketball or even the simplest games of skill. Tom and James were tremendous athletes. James could catch, shoot, and hit better than just about anyone I knew—and he was born deaf. To compensate for his handicap, James used his intelligence. Boy, was he smart. But while we did all we could to help him be social, it wasn't enough. So, when I was just ten and James sixteen, we drove up to Jackson, Mississippi, to a school for the deaf and settled James into his new home. We were devastated to leave him behind. But the school turned out to be a great thing, and James soon learned sign language and made all kinds of friends. He would return to Crawford to work with my father in the bricklaying business. Despite not being able to hear or speak, James was a legitimate bricklayer, earning the real money, while most of us—his siblings—were merely helpers.

As a child and a teenager, I was very shy. I didn't have that many friends and spent a great deal of time on my own, playing sports, reading books, and running. I ran everywhere: from our home to school and back; from Crawford to the country. Some days I would just run on random paths to see where they would take me. This was before I played sports in high school so I wasn't doing it to get in shape for the season and I certainly wasn't going to be a marathoner. Twenty-six miles is a *long* way in Mississippi heat. I just ran. "Run, Forrest, run!" It's an oft-quoted line from the 1994 film *Forrest Gump,* in which a young man, after having leg braces removed, just runs and runs and runs. As an adult, he runs across America, not really sure why or where he was going. If the movie had come out back when I was a kid, they would have nicknamed me Forrest. I ran with no real purpose or goal. I just enjoyed running. I didn't need a stopwatch or a team tryout or any other goal to motivate me on those hot July days back in Mississippi.

Since I didn't play sports initially in school, I wasn't allowed to use the track or the workout facilities at school. We didn't have any money to buy weights so I lifted tire rims in an empty room in our house. I would find a pole and attach rims on both ends to serve as a barbell. I didn't really know why I worked out so much. Maybe because I watched bodybuilders on television and was impressed with the way they looked? Maybe if I looked like them I'd have more friends and attention from girls? Even I was a little vain. But I really think I ran without a goal in mind.

Goals are good things to have, make no mistake, and I set short-term and long-term goals routinely. But I don't believe you have to have a goal to get going. We are all different and have unique assets that we bring to the table. How we use those assets determines how successful we are. A problem I have with goals is how they are set. Plateau goals to me are levels—like statistics. I am going to run a mile in six minutes or bake two hundred cookies or sell forty cell phones. They set the bar for you but what happens if you run the mile in 6:01 or bake 198 cookies or sell thirty-eight cell phones? Are you a failure? Of course not.

I DIDN'T HAVE THAT many goals, in school or in life, when I entered the student body at B. L. Moor High School. Moor was small, with about twenty-five kids in each class from some of the poorer communities in Oktibbeha County. Many of our classes were held in trailers, as the original school building was outdated and too small. School was okay for me, something I knew I had to do, even though my parents often had to push me to do my homework. Math, English, science, and the like never really took a liking to me, nor I to them. I did enjoy auto shop class because I enjoyed working with my hands and putting together engines from scrap. As I worked on engine parts and calibrators, I recall my mind wandering back then, thinking about the future. What else was out there in the world besides Mississippi and bricklaying? I knew I didn't want that to be my future, and soon destiny came calling.

One day in early September of my sophomore year of high school, 1978, I decided to play hooky with a friend, despite the fear of getting caught and whipped by my father. We snuck out of class to make our way off campus. Suddenly, the school principal, Mr. Ezell Wickes, spotted us. He and I made eye contact before we bolted. Mr. Wickes never caught up to us but seeing that this was a small school, he easily recognized my face and clothing. Suffice to say, I knew what I had coming when I returned. He had a big old leather strap in his office and he gave me five hard hits with it. It was painful.

But Mr. Wickes witnessed how fast I had sprinted away from him, and realized my speed could be put to good use to keep me out of trouble. So he forced me to meet with Charles Davis, the head football coach at B. L. Moor. After an initial conversation between us, him doing most of the talking, he convinced me to try out for the football team. My mother was against it initially, as she was concerned about my body, and she also knew that my shyness might be a liability in such a rough game—shyness in that I didn't like confrontation and never seemed very aggressive. (And she thought basketball was my future, anyway.) As for my father, he seemed indifferent, more concerned with bricklaying and providing for the family. My older brother Tom was already a high school football star so it wasn't that my parents didn't know what the sport was all about—the violent hits, the summer workouts, the emphasis on football from local townspeople, as it was *the* thing to do on Friday nights. As for me, if I was going to play, it wasn't good enough just to be average. I had to be great. The only way I knew how to do anything was to outwork, outperform, and outplay everyone else. Even though my father wasn't there watching, I felt he was, and I didn't want to disappoint him.

Coach Davis knew when to be tough but also when to show compassion. I immediately took a liking to him as tryouts began. I wasn't scared, though I knew the other guys had an advantage over me because they had played organized football before. I wanted the guys to accept me. The best way I thought I could do that was to work hard and get good—fast.

It took me a while to learn the game of football. I watched the older guys on the team and copied how they practiced and how they played. Not only was I still impressed by the little quarterback, Kent Thomas, but I idolized Lester Tate, a bulky running back who had speed and grace. He was the man on the field and popular in the school hallways.

Both Kent and Lester had style. They had something in their attitude that personified confidence. It wasn't arrogance; it was a complete presentation of how they looked, how they practiced, and how they approached every game. Presentation is everything and it's something that I have lived by every day since. (More on that later.)

The high school team practiced and played on a field that was more dirt than grass, surrounded by barely a hundred seats with stadium lights on one side. The helmets and pads and uniforms were in poor condition. The upperclassmen and starters got the "best" equipment, and by best I mean the least torn up. Pants, shoes, and socks were all in very limited supply. Not having much made me want more. If there was money in the school to spend, and there wasn't much, it tended to go toward things like books and classroom materials.

I worked hard in tryouts and was fortunate enough to make the team as a tenth grader, despite my rookie tendencies, like running the wrong route, dropping easy balls, and even putting on my pads the wrong way. When it came to the season, though, I played sparingly as a kick returner and, occasionally, as a defensive back and receiver. Because of my size, lanky build, good hands, and speed, returning kicks and playing receiver and defensive back seemed like a good fit. Speed was necessary to be a running back, but at six foot one, I was just too tall and I certainly didn't know enough about the game to be a quarterback. I didn't quite have the game or the techniques down, but I was in great condition. True to form, after a tough practice I would run the ten miles or so back home.

Coach Davis used to run us up and down hills every day after practice as either a form of conditioning or punishment, forty yards up, and forty yards down. Guys would be throwing up on the way up *and* down. I remember after practice one day I decided to run some more hills to get in better condition on my own. I started up the slope, sweating profusely in the hot August sun of Mississippi, and said, "I give up." I was so tired and hot I walked back down the hill and headed to the locker room to hang it up for the day. But then the voices in my head started to talk. "Never quit!" I kept hearing over and over again. I stopped walking, turned around, and started running the hills again.

Before the following season, my junior year, I knew what I needed to do to get better; I worked hard in the off season to get faster and stronger. I watched the upperclassmen as I waited for my opportunity. Some summer days I would be up at dawn, work all day long with my father and brothers laying brick, get dropped off at school for practice, and then have to run the ten miles home because I had no ride. The run home was often in pitch darkness and the route took me along woods. It was silent and dark and the littlest sounds from the woods scared me to death. So I would pick up my pace.

I had to be the best and had to prove myself to Coach Davis and to my teammates. Maybe that came from always wanting to please my father. As a result, my junior year was my breakout season. I focused on playing receiver and defensive back, and playing one position helped me play the other. I learned how to run routes and how to cover, how to receive and how to intercept, but mostly, I just relied on instinct and reacted to my opponent. Our team won games and I started to shine on the field, scoring touchdowns and smothering opponents on defense.

I was still very shy, avoiding crowds and girls, and I only had one or two buddies with whom I occasionally hung out. I was comfortable as a loner and didn't let anyone get close to me. I was so used to being alone that it was comforting to me just to be on my own. (I still am somewhat of a loner today.) But classmates and teachers started to notice me more, as I became more of a leader and star on the football field. I have to admit, it was nice to have classmates approach me and say, "Good job" after a Friday game. But it wasn't satisfying for me the way I had hoped. I thought if I excelled on the field and gained recognition from classmates, it would make me feel whole. I was wrong. I did like being part of a team, as it allowed me to feel that I fit in somewhere, but a big piece of me still felt like a loner. My parents were supportive of my game and efforts, and always tried to be there for every game, though my mother cringed every time I took a lick on the field, something she never got used to.

Though my stardom blossomed, and I came to love playing football, I did give other sports a try, competing in the high jump on the track team and playing forward on the Moor High School basketball team. I wasn't a typical high jumper, who approached the bar, twisted, and turned my body before leaping backward over the bar and landing on my back. No, I just leapt and straddled the bar, landing on my feet. My first year on the track team, one of our stars was entered in so many events, our coach replaced him with me in the anchor leg of the team relay. For those of you not familiar with a track relay, each team has four runners, and each runner runs one lap around the track after being passed a baton from a teammate. Typically, the fastest runner runs the last or anchor lap. Well, on this particular day in the late 1970s, I was the anchor runner and was handed the baton with about a twenty to thirty yard lead on the next closest team. I was home free! I bolted out and burned out. I got sucked up by the runner behind me who blew past and won the race for his team. After I crossed the finish line, I remember collapsing onto my knees, dehydrated and exhausted. I had let my team down and failed.

It took me many more years to recognize that I couldn't win at everything. Abraham Lincoln lost elections before becoming our great president. Henry Ford went bankrupt before creating the automobile empire that bears his name. Babe Ruth failed to get a hit the majority of times he came to the plate. Michael Jordan missed twice as many shots as he made. If those at the top of their profession don't win in everything all the time, I think it's safe to say that neither will we.

Regardless of my failures on the track, it was football that drove me and moved me, a game that was my great escape. As my athleticism improved and I found myself with a more complete skill set, it began to occur to me that football could be my way out of Mississippi and the only life I knew. But my brother had thought this way, too.

# The Satellite Express

Although I was close to all my brothers and sisters, particularly my brothers, I had the most in common with my older brother, Tom. Not only were we close in age, but he was always keen on sports and we could often be found playing sandlot football or stickball or some invented sports game outside, like tennis baseball where we'd swing with a bat at a tennis ball. Tom grew to be six foot two, 275 pounds—even bigger than our father.

His tremendous size helped him excel on the high school football field, and won him the attention of college coaches and the acclaim of the community. Tom was a decent student—not great—but as with football, he always gave his best effort when it came to academics, and ultimately, he decided to attend nearby Jackson State in Jackson, Mississippi. He starred as a center on their offensive line. What Tom may have lacked in size in relation to those big boys, he made up for with heart and talent. So much so that he, along with many teammates, coaches, friends, and family, thought he was headed for a professional career in the NFL. He was excited by the prospect and said the first thing he wanted to do with his initial NFL paycheck was to build my parents a new home. That's what drove him.

My mother admits now that she always believed that Tom would be the one to make it big, not me, to live in a world unknown to all of us at the time. Sadly, Tom never made it to that world and never played a down in the National Football League. I guess NFL teams thought he was undersized to play center and they certainly didn't give much credence to a small-sized player coming out of Jackson State (even though Walter Payton made it from Jackson). He never got that big first paycheck and never built my parents a new home.

Not only did Tom fail to get drafted, he didn't even get a tryout with an NFL team. He had put all of his eggs in one basket. As far as he was concerned, he was going to play football professionally and never even considered any alternative. These unfortunate circumstances taught me more than anything else to always have a backup plan. It is important to have dreams, but you can never have such tunnel vision that you ignore the reality that sometimes we all come up short. But you know what? I admire Tom because he gave it his all. He gave everything he had to the game of football and taught me that you'll never know unless you try, a motto that I have kept with me for decades. He's right. Failure is just part of life. You fail, you move on.

I recall a conversation I had with Tom when I was just starting out in college a few years after him. He didn't know what to do with his life, since a career in the NFL was no longer a reality. (He became a high school football coach soon after.) But he did know what *I* had to do. "You have to do it; it's in your hands now," he said to me with an intense stare while grabbing my elbow. I knew what he meant. The future was on my shoulders. He was passing the torch of responsibility to make things better for our family, to build the new house; to get out of Mississippi; to make a better life. I wasn't so sure how I was going to do that, I just knew it was my destiny. I wasn't going to be a bricklayer.

I took away something else from Tom's path and his failure to make it to the NFL: the necessity of doubt. As I blossomed as a football player, people would tell me about the riches of the NFL but I never bought into the hype, knowing what the expectations had done to Tom. So by my senior year in high school, when the colleges started calling and writing, I was very wary. Playing at such a small high school out in the country of Mississippi, I didn't get a lot of personal attention from college recruiters, but I did receive letters from UCLA, USC, and from close-by LSU, and the famed running schools of Mississippi State (MSU) and Jackson State. Though MSU was just forty-five minutes away in Starkville, their system of play, relying on the running back, didn't seem like a good fit for me as a wide receiver. Tom had the connection with Jackson State, but he acknowledged that I wouldn't fit in their system either as they, too, relied on the running game. I wanted to be an important part of my team's offensive strategy. I was impressed by the powerhouse schools on the west coast and by LSU, but the school that impressed me most was Mississippi Valley State.

Two things sold me on the relatively obscure Division I-AA school in Itta Bena. First, the coach, Archie Cooley, loved to have his team throw the football, and second, they were the only school to send a coach to watch me play in person. Coach Cooley had heard about me through a network of black high school coaches and he told me I would be unstoppable at MVS.

At Coach Cooley's invitation, I went to visit Mississippi Valley that fall. I liked the team colors (green, red, and white) and was instantly taken in by the whole atmosphere with the raucous band and good-looking cheerleaders. I was a nerd and, boy, did the women at Valley look good. When an assistant coach traveled to Moor to watch me play in a game, I looked him in the eye afterward and I could tell he was an honest man. I gave him a handshake agreement to play at MVS.

My football career at Moor High School finished with All-State honors as a receiver and as a defensive back. In my senior season, I caught eighty-eight passes in ten games, helping the team to an 18–2 record in over two full seasons. Graduation came quickly and I was excited to be moving on to a new phase in my life. Though I would be two and a half hours from home, I was close enough to visit often and had teammates from high school attending MVS with me. Before I left for training camp the summer before freshman year, my mother left me with some sage advice: "Son, you better be good and don't get in any trouble. Oh, and don't get those girls pregnant." It was classic Mom. My father didn't offer any great words of wisdom, but I did see the look on his face when I left, a sense of sadness that I was leaving, though he would never say it.

Itta Bena was a big city compared to Crawford. It was the hometown of legendary blues player B. B. King as well as home to Mississippi Valley State College. The football stadium at MVS held ten thousand fans. The practice fields were littered with mosquitoes and dirt patches, but right after the start of my first practice, I felt that the risk I had taken in choosing tiny MVS was the right one. Archie Cooley was nicknamed the "Gunslinger" because of how often he had his quarterbacks sling the ball. This was a coach who ran a no-huddle offense, who called for a pass play 90 percent of the time, and whose quarterbacks routinely threw fifty to sixty passes a game. That's my kind of coach. Archie lived up to his nickname in every way. He wore flashy clothes and a big cowboy hat. When he walked into a room, he wanted the room to notice.

As was typical then—and is now—freshmen athletes attended summer school and orientation on campus before the regular school year began. That first summer, two of my good buddies from high school, quarterback Willie Gillispie and tackle Joe Thomas, joined me at Valley. But they never quite liked it and decided to leave even before our first training camp. I remember watching them get on a Greyhound bus to go home, wondering if I should be on the bus with them. I missed the security of being home but I didn't get on the bus. MVS was part of my journey to a better life, and I wouldn't lose sight of that.

My freshman year, I just tried to keep my head down and my mouth closed and to work hard. I knew there were teammates more talented than me, but I vowed that no one would outwork me. I was also very coachable, willing to take criticism from coaches and veteran players and tinker with my technique. My receivers' coach, Gloster Richardson, had played in the NFL, and taught me everything I needed to know about catching a football: how to watch it come out of the QB's hands, how to cradle the ball against your body and how to make that quick first step after a catch. I soaked up everything I could. For one pass route for a wide receiver, I might learn five different ways to run it. Too many of us turn a deaf ear to criticism because of ego, even when we know it is warranted, but I was always willing to listen if it would make me a better player. Freshman year, 1981, I had thirty catches and scored two touchdowns. Generally not great statistics, but it was a start and, just as things had improved dramatically between my first two seasons in high school, I would make adjustments so history might repeat itself.

One thing that hit me that first season was the varying degrees of work ethic on a team. There were some guys who gave 100 percent every day in practice and others who just exerted enough effort to get by. It pissed me off. I couldn't understand how anybody could *not* give an all-out effort daily. And I'm talking off the field as well. Being early or on time for meetings, arriving home before curfew, being on the team bus well before departure. As I matured, gained confidence, and became more of a leader at MVS in succeeding years, I had no problem confronting those who I believed were "phoning it in," and would continue to do so in the NFL. My fellow receivers at Valley worked hard but didn't put in the extra effort. They weren't totally committed. They didn't spend the time in the weight room after practice or after home games as a few of us did.

I was happy to be playing football at MVS and satisfied with the college life experience that first year and, though I focused on football and academic classes, I still found time to go to a few parties along the way. My teammates soon began to trust me as the one guy who would watch over everyone else—the designated driver, if you will. I didn't mind. It fit my personality. I did join a fraternity, Phi Beta Sigma, and I made some friends instantly.

Sophomore year, Willie Totten became my Joe Montana at Mississippi Valley. Willie was a red-shirt freshman (a sophomore in school but an athlete with four years of eligibility remaining) who had such a big heart and a desire to get better and to win. He was also willing to sacrifice to do it, something he and I shared. He was hungry like me. We quickly became friends off the field—and unstoppable on it. We worked together before practice and late into the evenings after. We worked on our routes, our timing, the height of the ball, our snap count, and just about every other aspect of the quarterback–wide receiver tandem. The work paid off. We ran a stack four offense, meaning we lined up four wide receivers on one side of the field. Between Willie's passing (he was nicknamed "Satellite") and the receiving corps catching, we earned the nickname the "Satellite Express" because the ball was seemingly in orbit all of the time. In 1982, I more than doubled my number of catches to sixty-six and scored seven touchdowns, not to mention gaining over a thousand receiving yards, thanks to Willie. (Willie would later return to Mississippi Valley State to coach after stints in the Canadian Football League and, briefly, in the NFL. In the summer of 2005, I had the chance to return to my alma mater on an invitation from Willie to work with the players on the MVS fields, which are still full of dirt and mosquitoes.)

Despite my sudden success, I never looked at myself as the BMOC—Big Man On Campus. While majoring in electronics and earning a B average, it was warming to receive pats on the back from students and praise from fans, but I was still the shy kid from Crawford. In the shell of a helmet and uniform, I was in my comfort zone. When I could put on the equipment and just play, I could be myself, but away from football I felt bare.

No matter how many touchdowns I scored, I still didn't have a lot of money and the meals we were given at MVS were not enough for a growing man. Many late nights I would go over to the home of a teammate, Maurice Wade, and we'd cook pancakes and eat hearty meals together as Maurice always had money for food. He wasn't rich but he had food. I knew I didn't want to live like this— relying on others for food. It drove me even harder to succeed.

Things exploded during my junior year when we went 7–2–1, when I had 102 catches and fourteen touchdowns, earning the nickname "World" because I seemed to catch anything that was thrown my way. In one game in October 1983, I caught twenty-four passes against Southern University. I even earned All-American honors. But I never really celebrated the accomplishments and, in fact, I thought I could do better. So I just worked harder. To talent evaluators in the NFL, my stock apparently was rising. Maybe I could get drafted and build my parents that house? Tom's disappointment was still fresh in my mind.

By senior year, things were crazy and tough, trying to balance football and school, and trying to keep my head clear from family and friends and teammates who said I'd be an NFL superstar—and from those who said I wouldn't measure up. Agents began trying to sign me for their own financial benefit and Coach Cooley did his best to educate me on the agent process. Agents would go after my family, my teammates, and my coaches to try to get to me. They tried to bribe Coach Cooley, promising him money if he could convince me to sign with them. Whenever a coach tries to steer a player to an agent, something isn't right. But all along, I wanted to sign with a black agent. I wanted to give a black agent the opportunity to do something big. So I decided to go with Eric Glenn, an agent out of Oakland, whose clients included Willie Gault.

During my senior season, I'd often play head games with myself, at times convincing myself that I could be great at the pro level while at other times pointing out to myself all the "great" players who never made it, including my brother. But the best thing I could do was to let my play speak for itself. In 1984, Mississippi Valley State went 9–2 and we averaged over fifty-eight points per game. Carl Byrum, who would later play for the Buffalo Bills, was at fullback and Joe Thomas, who would later be drafted by the Denver

Broncos, lined up at wide receiver alongside me. That season, I had 112 catches, 1,845 receiving yards, and 28 touchdowns, including one quarter against Kentucky State when I caught twelve passes and made three TDs! I led the nation in catches and receiving yards and set eighteen I-AA records along the way, while earning All-American honors for a second time. I even finished ninth in the Heisman Trophy voting! But a playoff loss to Louisiana Tech dampened the year for me. I cried like a baby after the game. I wanted to win a championship at MVS so badly. I was devastated after the loss and by the sudden realization that my collegiate career was over.

But I soon realized I had to turn my attention to my professional future. As wintertime approached, the NFL Draft talk heated up. Now, despite what many considered an outstanding senior season, I wasn't inundated with media requests nor did I get much mention by draft experts. I think people decided that since I played at a small I-AA school in Mississippi, I did what I did against weak competition and couldn't handle playing at the professional level. Obviously, I disagreed, and it made me want to prove myself that much more to those who believed a small-school player just wasn't good enough. In fact, I took it upon myself to represent all the "little school" guys. I knew if I could get drafted and make it in the NFL, it would open many more doors in the future for talented players from lesser-known schools. There were many disadvantages to playing at such an obscure school at the I-AA level—drawbacks I had been aware of when I signed up in 1980.

For one thing, we received very little media attention and our games were not televised, so scouts, reporters, and media draft experts rarely saw us play during the season. For another, MVS didn't have a lot of money, which meant we didn't have a sophisticated video equipment system to make all sorts of fancy video highlights to send out to scouts and the media. So when an NFL scout did come to Itta Bena, I'd make sure I did everything possible to sell myself. I'd sit in the film room with them as they watched me on tape, pointing out things I thought put me in a good light and let them fire away with questions like, "What would you do in this situation?" or "What were you thinking when you saw that defense?" I was always my worst critic and used these rare opportunities to receive some great advice from the pro scouts about what I could have done better on routes or in my technique.

I MENTIONED THAT 1984 was crazy, but it didn't all have to do with football, agents, or the NFL. A big part of it had to do with basketball—sort of. Since I was friendly with some of the MVS hoops players, I went to as many home games as possible and, at one particular game, I noticed a beautiful young woman seated nearby. Her name was Jackie Mitchell and she was part of a senior high school group on campus visiting MVS. It turned out that after touring the campus in the afternoon, the group decided to stay for the basketball game. Jackie was hot! Great hair, perfect skin, and a killer body. Some of Jackie's friends and a few Mississippi Valley coeds were making a bit of a fuss over me (embarrassing me, admittedly) and when I decided to approach her, we didn't hit it off at first—or second, for that matter. Jackie couldn't understand why everyone was making such a big deal over me. She had no idea who I was or that I was a pretty good football player and she really didn't care. But my persistence paid off as she ultimately gave me her phone number. I told her I would call her at noon the following day and, like I've always been, I was early, calling her at 11:58 a.m.

We began to date casually, and soon I was making the sixty-minute drive from Itta Bena to her home in Greenville two or three times a week, occasionally bringing flowers and gifts, trying to woo her.

Jackie was very close with her two sisters, Toni and Marilyn, and her mother, Gloria, who wasn't too happy to hear that Jackie liked a senior in college. In fact, her mother told her she couldn't date me because I was too old. And this despite Jackie telling her mom that I was just twenty, when I was really twenty-two!

There was a boy who lived down the street from Jackie and her mother in their hometown of Greenville, Mississippi, who Gloria thought was more appropriately aged—and what's more, she knew his parents. For Gloria, knowing a boy's parents meant knowing the boy, and my parents lived three hours away, which back in Mississippi was a cross-country trip. She tried to break us up as we began dating, and she had never even met me! But the first time I met Gloria everything changed. When I arrived at her house, I took a seat in the living room while Jackie went into a back bedroom to get her mom. When Gloria entered the living room, I immediately stood up, extended a hand and asked her simply, "How are you doing, Mrs. Mitchell?" Well, the way Gloria tells it, even with three daughters, she never once had a boyfriend stand up when she entered a room or ask how she was doing. This won her over (that, and perhaps the fact that she thought I looked like a tall fifteen-year-old, which made the age difference easier to swallow).

Like her daughter, Gloria only followed local high school and big-time college football so she had no idea about local college Mississippi Valley State football. She certainly didn't know much about me—and I liked that.


In the weeks and days leading up to the April 1985 NFL Draft, I received all kinds of predictions and input about where I would be drafted. Some believed that I would be picked in the first round, while others thought I wouldn't be drafted at all. Maybe I was headed to Indianapolis or Dallas or Green Bay? But I didn't care where I went, as long as I went. I knew my play stood on its own but I also knew there were questions about the competition level and about my time in the forty-yard dash: 4.6 seconds, which to some NFL scouts was slow for a wide receiver; they wanted to see a 4.3 or 4.4 time. I still maintain my slower time was because no one ever taught me the proper sprinting technique with arms close to the body, back upright, etc.

On draft day, I didn't hold a big bash for family and friends like many potential draft picks do. I didn't want to be the guy sitting around with nothing to celebrate. I honestly still thought as late as the day of the draft that I might not even get picked. That's how much doubt I held inside. So on that day, I went over to my brother Tom's apartment in Jackson, Mississippi, and sat down to watch the NFL Draft on ESPN with Tom and his wife. At the time, Tom was coaching football at a nearby high school. He had been with me through everything, a big part of my high school and college career, and I wanted him to be a part of the big day.

As the selections began, the mood was surreal. I realized that people whom I didn't know, living thousands of miles away, had total control of my life at that moment. They would decide if I would make it and where I would be living, not me. Having your destiny out of your control is a very uneasy feeling and I suddenly didn't like it. As the picks began, two wide receivers were selected: Al Toon and Eddie Brown. There was a flurry of draft maneuvering as teams tried to trade up for higher slots, and the San Francisco 49ers were on the move.

What I didn't know at the time was that 49ers head coach Bill

Walsh was well aware of me. The previous season, in October 1984, as he sat and watched college football highlights in his Houston hotel room on a Saturday night before his Niners played the Houston Oilers, he had caught a glimpse of some of my highlight catches from our game that day and was impressed. Impressed enough to watch me closely as I participated in the annual Blue-Grey game, an All-Star game for college seniors, in which I was named MVP. Impressed enough that Walsh didn't listen to San Francisco scouts who told him I couldn't play at the NFL level. Impressed enough to orchestrate a draft day trade, giving up first, second, and third round picks to the New England Patriots to move up from the twenty-eighth pick to the sixteenth in the first round. Walsh was concerned the Dallas Cowboys, who picked before him, would get me before the 49ers' pick at twenty-eighth.

So as San Francisco was on the clock and the world awaited their decision, I received a call at Tom's home from the 49ers, telling me they were about to take me with their first round pick. I could barely speak. I was going to play for the defending Super Bowl champions and for legendary Bill Walsh in the classiest organization in football. I immediately thought of all the great players on the team—Joe Montana, Roger Craig, Ronnie Lott, and Dwight Clark. The San Francisco 49ers! I knew that Joe had played at Notre Dame and Ronnie was a USC Trojan and that many 49ers had played at the highest levels in college. I was in awe, as I had watched these soon-to-be legends play on television. They epitomized for me what football was all about: the love of the game, the professional approach, and the desire to win. I had just wanted to go *somewhere* but this was a perfect situation.

Tom and I didn't jump around and celebrate; I think we were in shock. *Did it actually just happen?* We immediately made plans to get me to the airport to fly to San Francisco, even before calling my mom and dad to tell them the good news.

But I didn't realize that Mom had been able to watch the draft. In those days, to earn some extra money for the family, my mother would clean the homes of wealthier families, and on draft day I knew she was busy doing just that. But the lady of that particular house on this particular day knew who I was and what a big day it was for our family, and she insisted that my mother sit in front of the television and watch. It must have been a big thrill for Mom. My father, like most days, was out in the heat, laying down bricks.

Jackie was still in high school at the time so she instructed Gloria to watch ESPN all day. She said she would call Gloria from school at ten a.m. to get an update. So Gloria did as instructed and watched ESPN for the first time ever. It wasn't that long before my name was called. One problem. As the ESPN commentators talked about me, they mentioned my school, position, and my age, which was twenty-two years old! Remember, young Jackie had told her mother that I was only twenty. Thankfully, years later, we can laugh about it.

We were all excited that I had been drafted but deep inside, secretly, I still had my doubts. Could I compete at the NFL level, particularly with the reigning Super Bowl champions? How could I survive in such a big city when all I had known were the fields of Mississippi? Would I fail in the NFL and have to face my old friends and family and become a bricklayer in Mississippi? Before I would know the answer to these big questions, I had to face one fear that had nothing to do with football or San Francisco.

# The Rookie

THE REALITY WAS THAT I was more scared to board the airplane to San Francisco than I was to play with the Super Bowl champions. I had never been on a plane, only seen them fly overhead or on television. I was seated in a window seat and as the plane lifted off the ground, I was crumbling inside. The ground was moving away so fast and there was nothing I could do about it! I closed my eyes and just waited for the bumps to stop. It was intense for the first part of the trip. There was a man seated next to me but I didn't talk to him, as I didn't want to let on that I was scared.

When I exited the plane at San Francisco airport, the flashbulbs started going off, the cameras began to roll, and microphones popped into my face. I was not accustomed to, nor expecting, a media avalanche at the airport. I hadn't dealt with many reporters at Mississippi Valley State so this was like a surprise southern summer thunderstorm. I knew people were staring at me, and it made me uncomfortable. I also wasn't great at answering questions, as I kept stumbling over my words. (So much so that my new agent soon thereafter had me go to a speech coach, but after only two meetings with the therapist, I stopped going. I was trying to be someone else—trying to appear cool and fit in—but I was just fooling myself.)

Keep in mind that there were many Niners fans and members of the media who not only criticized my being picked but questioned Bill Walsh's sanity for orchestrating the pick. From what I read in the papers and heard on the radio, there were many expecting me, even wanting me, to fail, but that just gave me more reason to go out there and excel. A few weeks after my initial press conference in San Francisco, I returned to begin mini-camp with the rookies and veterans. I was like a deer in the headlights, initially too stunned to say anything to Joe or Roger or Dwight. At the first full team meeting, Coach Walsh had each of the rookies stand up. He introduced us and asked the team to welcome us into the 49ers family. We then broke off into position meetings and I finally had the chance to meet Dwight, Freddie Solomon, and the other receivers, who were all very open and kind. But you really didn't get to know your teammates in meetings or at practice; it was after practice and during lunch that you had the chance to really talk. Freddie was great with his stories about the past!

I roomed that first training camp with Shawn Rogers, a running back from the University of California–Davis. Shawn pegged me as a country boy; I pegged him as west coast. We got along just fine, as his laid-back attitude and maturity helped me. We were both competitive by nature and found a variety of sports to compete in— basketball, tennis, track, etc. We were kind of like Dan Jansen and

Dave O'Brien, the two world-class triathletes who became famous through those "Dan vs. Dave" Reebok commercials in 1992, in which they challenged each other to a variety of events. Shawn was a good guy and helped me get through those first few weeks at camp at Sierra College in Sacramento. He was from the area and we would often go over to his house and have dinner with his wife to get away from football for a while. Unfortunately, he was released at the end of training camp and never played football again. It was hard to see him go since I would be staying. (We remain the best of friends and have entered into many business partnerships together. Shawn is currently a sergeant in the Sacramento Police Department.)

From my first few days with the 49ers, I took an immediate liking to Roger Craig. Roger was all about hard work. I knew that before the plane landed in the Bay Area. Roger had heart and was durable, taking hits and getting right back up. But watching him work out was truly something to see. To him, the game was all about speed, and his conditioning drills were evidence of that. Roger would do sprints on the track, run cone drills for lateral and backward speed, run through ropes set over tires on grass fields, and do just about anything that he thought could help him get faster. He invited me to join him in workouts before training camp and I refused at first. Though it was nice of him to ask, I was well aware of the strenuous workouts Roger was known for and I didn't want to embarrass myself. When I did decide to join him for a run up a two-and-a-half-mile hill, I could barely keep up. After the first day, I actually quit, thinking there was no way I could participate at this level and so I avoided the workouts for a few weeks. But ultimately, of course, quitting just wasn't an option and after Roger kept pestering me, eventually I returned and earned my stripes, even earning applause from my fellow workout partners when I made it to the top of the hill.

Remember that I was clocked at a "slow" 4.6 forty-yard dash leading up to the draft, so I certainly needed to improve my speed. But there's a big difference between being fast and having football speed. Football speed is how crisp you come out of running routes, how quickly you can "stop on a dime" and change direction, and how quickly you break off the line of scrimmage when the ball is snapped. The faster you can do all of these, the greater the advantage you have on the man covering you. Football speed can be learned through hard work and, after years of working on the track, I actually got *faster* as the years went on. Joe Montana was always amazed at how I was able to get past defenders who were faster than I. *That's* football speed.

On the practice field in San Francisco, the veterans were gracious enough to give me pointers about how routes are run or how balls are caught. The vets nicknamed me "Fifi" because of my haircut, a cut that was very short on the sides and high up top. I always tried to do something a little different. I didn't like the nickname, though. I especially hated it when they called me Fifi during meetings. They were willing, however, to share and I was willing to listen, something you don't find today in the NFL. Veterans are more concerned with their careers, and rookies, flush with rich contracts, think they know it all. Before the start of the 2005 season, I was surprised to hear some of the comments that Green Bay Packers quarterback Brett Favre made when asked about mentoring newly drafted quarterback Aaron Rodgers. Favre insisted that he didn't get paid to coach the game to young guys, that it was not in his contract and that he wouldn't go out of his way to tutor Rodgers. Little does Brett know that everything he does in practice, during games, with the media, and in the training room will be mimicked by Rodgers anyway. Joe Montana knew it. Favre should have known better. I think if he could take his words back now, he would.

The 49ers veterans taught me a lot about the game including the *business* of playing the game. I remember riding in a car with Dwight Hicks, Dwight Clark, and Ronnie Lott on the way to a 49ers luncheon after practice one day and the vets gave me a warning (I can't remember exactly who said it): "You are going to see so much happen in this game—the business side of things, the politics—but you have to be able to focus and concentrate on what you do best." I learned that lesson well, particularly as the 49ers dynasty began to break up in the early 1990s. It doesn't matter how good you are or what your loyalty is to a team. Professional football is a business and you will get replaced. I saw it up close when Roger Craig, Ronnie Lott, and Joe Montana departed. I saw the business side of football on the field, when occasionally players wouldn't go all out for fear of injury and thus jeopardizing their value on the free agent market. It was a business back when I broke in and it has grown tenfold since.

PEOPLE, EVEN TODAY, ask me about Joe Montana. He is such a legend to football fans around the world. They want to know what he was really like, if he ever got scared, how he was able to win so many games. The Joe that I came to know was as cool as they say, calm and collected, the type of guy that could fit in, in any room, giving off an aura of approachability. Early in that first training camp, and in the first few weeks of the season, Joe and I had some flashes of unique chemistry in practice. The savvy vet told me he saw some talent in me and liked the way I ran my routes and made big plays—in practice. (Years later, Joe would thank me for helping prolong his career, noting that I made life easier for him the way I played, by running precise routes, catching almost anything he threw, and taking hits across the middle of the field.) But despite our connection, we never really bonded off the field. I mean, we were friendly and gracious working out together in the facility or over lunch, but outside of football, we didn't hang out socially. I really didn't hang with any of my teammates. It somewhat surprised me that players on the team didn't seem to spend time together. Occasionally, if there was a party or a celebration, we would all get together but never just because. Maybe we were all too focused on football. It probably comes as a surprise to 49ers fans that we weren't so tight away from the field, but we certainly were a family when it came to football.

And there was Bill Walsh, aka "The Genius." I had had my first conversation with Coach Walsh right before the 49ers announced their pick on draft day, when he told me I was their guy and that he was excited to have me on board. Soon after learning that he had stuck his neck out there for me, I felt an obligation to prove him right. He saw something in me before I even got to San Francisco that no one else had. I had heard stories about Coach being a football genius and, at least from the day I met him, he was. There was just something in his brain that allowed him to think a step or two ahead of everyone else. He revolutionized the game of football with his west coast offensive scheme, a new system of short passes and multiple receivers, but he did more than that.

For me, Bill was like a father. I could talk to him about football, about relationships, about the business of being a professional athlete. He even had the same body language of disapproval that my own father had: that stern look, that crossing of the arms, that raised eyebrow. It said it all to me. I never wanted to let my father down and now I never wanted to let Bill down. He knew when to turn on the emotion, when to keep it light and when to raise his voice. And did I mention that he was a true genius?

Bill prohibited the true hazing of rookies, now commonplace in the NFL. We didn't have to stand on chairs and sing songs or do juvenile physical pranks, like eat mush, and we were never taped to a goalpost during training camp. Bill felt that stuff like that just took our focus away from football—and I agree. Anything that took energy away from practice and the games was simply an obstacle. We didn't escape scot-free however. We did have rookie chores. I had to carry the veteran receivers' shoulder pads from the locker room to the practice field and the rookies had to buy food to bring on the plane on road trips. But this I could handle.

One great rookie moment in the NFL is getting your first paycheck, and I knew there was one thing that I had to do right away: begin to build my parents a new home in Starkville, Mississippi— a promise I had made to Tom and to myself years before.

(During that first year and a few years beyond, I did buy some extravagant cars and attached personalized license plates to them like "World Rice" or "Flash80." Looking back, my fancy car phase was about curiosity for me, always wanting to know what driving the nice cars would be like, as many of us dream about as kids. And I wanted to fit in with my teammates, who all drove fancy cars.)

By the end of that first training camp, when some of the veteran defensive backs like Ronnie Lott, Eric Wright, Dwight Hicks, and Carlton Williamson had trouble covering me, I knew I was doing something right. I started the season behind Dwight Clark and Freddie Solomon on the depth chart, but Bill expected me to see some action. I remember running out of the tunnel for our first regular season game of 1985 against the Minnesota Vikings on the road. It's hard to explain the feeling of being surrounded by sixty thousand screaming fans. The big games I played in in college were certainly nothing like this. But amazingly, I wasn't nervous. I had been dreaming about this for a long time, and I got swept up in the emotion. I was lucky; only a select few got the chance to play in the NFL that season and I was one of them. I started to cry like a baby, right there on the sidelines before kickoff. I should have saved those tears.

As THE GAME—and the season—got under way, things didn't go so well for me. When I got my first professional shot at wide receiver, I ran crisp routes and was able to break free of defenders, but something started to happen that had never happened before: I dropped balls. In an exhibition game a few weeks prior to the season kickoff against Minnesota, I had dropped two wide open, sure touchdown passes against the Los Angeles Rams in L.A. I mean *wide open*! I ran deep post routes and was out there all by myself, just waiting for the ball to come close. I watched the ball come down out of its spiral but the seconds lasted hours and I tightened up; the ball hit my hands and bounced off. At first I just figured it was a freak accident but then there was another dropped ball and then another. And the drops didn't stop in the preseason. In the first eleven regular season games, I dropped eleven passes. (My first NFL touchdown catch came against Atlanta on a twenty-five-yard pass from Joe.)

The media began to question my ability and the 49ers' draft. Would I ever become a star or was I a bust? Newspaper columnists questioned my readiness to play in the NFL. I read every single word written about me. Some guys prefer to ignore the press, fearful of what might be written. Some guys *say* they don't read the papers or listen to talk radio but I know they're lying. I, admittedly, soak it all up. It even fuels me—drives me. I know it's not the best way to get motivated, but the more people doubt me, the more I want to prove them wrong. Nicknames like "Butterfingers" began to crop up and the word "bust" was used more often than I care to remember.

After some particularly bad games, I retreated to the locker room and sat on a stool and just cried in front of my teammates and coaches. I was embarrassed, but couldn't help myself. I was so disappointed in myself and felt like I was letting my teammates down. I remember against Kansas City dropping two easy passes in the first half of the game and bawling my eyes out at halftime. In the second half, though we were up by a wide margin, Bill Walsh had our quarterback, Matt Cavanaugh, throw me a simple eight-yard pass to boost my confidence. I finally caught the ball . . . and then promptly fumbled it. Jogging back to the huddle after dropping a pass is a jog that takes forever. It's like the fans are seeing through your soul.

One of the most difficult things for an athlete to endure is getting booed in his home stadium or arena, and that's just what happened to me during those early months at Candlestick Park in San Francisco. Fans would scream at me on the sidelines, yelling that I was a bust, and they would boo me after every dropped catch. But they had every right to boo. They rightfully had high expectations of me. I had to work through the negativity. Somehow, I had to find a way to catch the football again. It had been so easy for so many years and then *poof*! It was gone. I put even more work in at the practice facility, but there was still no guarantee that things would turn around come game time.

Luckily for me, I was on a team of supportive players and coaches. Joe and Dwight and the coaches kept telling me they would stick by me and to keep my head up—despite a few nasty looks from Joe after I dropped some of his passes. At one point, Bill even started me ahead of veteran Freddie Solomon in the hope that it would give me confidence and shake me out of the slump, but I soon found myself back on the bench. I realized years later that I was just so eager to make big plays to prove myself that I lost focus on the little things—like catching the ball. I was so concerned with what I did after the catch, I couldn't even *make* the catch. But there was something deeper.

Throughout this difficult period, I was constantly on the phone with Jackie, who was beginning her first year as a premed student at the University of Southern Mississippi in Hattiesburg, and whom I was missing terribly. She would read stories about how fans were booing me and she knew I needed more support. And, of course, she gave me words of encouragement, trying to keep my spirits up. Despite her busy academic schedule, she flew out to San Francisco for Halloween weekend in October and traveled to many of our games against NFC West foes like New Orleans and Atlanta. I missed her terribly. I felt more alone than I ever had that first season in San Francisco, but Jackie's support gave me the strength to face the adversity head on and to turn things around.

In addition to missing Jackie and my growing self-doubts, there was something else weighing on my mind. I had recently been burned by someone in a business relationship and was now in financial trouble.

It was about that time that Roger Craig and I started to bond. Roger was a guy from Mississippi, so we had a common thread. He earned my trust throughout camp and early in the season, more so than the other veterans, and he could sense something was going on in my life that was affecting my play. I spilled my guts to Roger, and he immediately offered his help. He set me up with his agent, Jim Steiner, who helped set my finances and taxes straight and put me on the right path. I've been with Jim ever since.

I had my doubts during the tough stretch, wondering if I really was good enough to play in the NFL. But believe it or not, doubts have helped me in my journey, doubts from those around me or doubts within me. We all have doubts about our abilities and chances for success but it's how we react to those doubts that matters. Yes, it would be nice if we had complete confidence in every decision or challenge we take on, but that's not reality. Even the most accomplished people in society have doubts. But they never let the doubts prevent them from succeeding; rather, they embrace them and use them as motivation. My doubts were still very much with me in early December 1985. The drops continued until one Monday night in December.

On the ninth, we were playing the Los Angeles Rams prime time on *Monday Night Football* in a key game in the Western Division title race. Before kickoff, I really felt relaxed, despite all that had happened. Something inside told me I was finally ready. And I was. In one of my more memorable games, I caught ten passes for 241 yards, including a sixty-six-yard touchdown catch. It was the Jerry Rice coming-out party. Unfortunately, we lost the game to the Rams and, wanting to win as much as anybody, I was stung. But I knew my performance that night had shown the fans and media my true potential. I admit I was relieved, but I was still eager to show how much more I could do.

From there, things just kept getting better as my confidence rushed back in a tidal wave. So much so that when I saw that I had a clear advantage over a defender, or blew by him multiple times, I let Joe know—"I can beat this guy." (It took me a few seasons to learn that Bill Walsh and the guys in the press box called the plays, not Joe!) I only started a total of four games in 1985 but I had forty-nine catches on the season for 927 yards and was gratified to be named the NFC Rookie of the Year at the end of the regular season. Being recognized as the top rookie was great, but what I *really* wanted was to play in the Super Bowl and to be invited to the NFL Pro Bowl in Hawaii.

In an NFC playoff game against the New York Giants, we lost 17–3. The season was over. We didn't make it to the Super Bowl and I wasn't invited to Hawaii. Still, I would give myself a B grade for my first year in the league. I had weathered the storm of criticism and boos to reach unexpected heights in the second half of the season. I knew what to expect my second year and I knew what I had to do to get better. But there was still something missing in my life, and she was two thousand miles away.

# Everything but Her

**I** SO MISSED JACKIE and though we talked every day, sometimes five or six times, late into the night, I wanted her close. When the University of Southern Mississippi let out for the summer, I flew to my home state and drove up to Hattiesburg in a new Porsche, rented a U-Haul trailer, and took Jackie's things home to Greenville. I drove the U-Haul; she drove the Porsche. We spent three weeks in Greenville and, though I had a hotel room nearby, I spent most of my time at Gloria's house. At some point in the middle of my stay, Jackie and I decided that she should come out to San Francisco with me for a short period in late May. Easier said than done. We had to get Gloria's blessing.

"No, you're not married!" was Jackie's mother's initial response to her plan to spend a few weeks with me in San Francisco in the summer of 1986.

But a friend of Gloria's convinced her that Jackie had been a model daughter for years, and that it was time now to let her do what she wanted. So Gloria relented after Jackie promised that she would go out to the west coast for three weeks, and then return to Mississippi for school, something that meant a lot to her mother.

Before we left for San Francisco, we first drove to Starkville to see my folks. Despite the progress of our relationship, Jackie had never met my parents. Maybe it was a timing thing; maybe I wanted them to be in their new home when she first met them; maybe it was my father. Jackie had heard the stories about how tough my father could be and she was nervous to meet him. But a surprising hug and a joke off the bat by Dad settled her down.

After a few weeks laughing, eating, and living in San Francisco, I asked Jackie to stay indefinitely. In addition to her interest in premed, I also knew she had aspirations to model and reminded her there were great modeling schools in the Bay Area. Though she was inclined to take me up on the offer, she knew her mother would kill her. Education was paramount in her family and not returning to school would break her mother's heart. Jackie was scared to ask her mother, but I wasn't. I knew in my heart that Jackie would be fine out in California so I had no problem asking Gloria. So I picked up the phone—while Jackie listened in on another phone—and, after promising that Jackie would finish school and get a degree, she gave in. I even offered Gloria a visit to San Francisco to see where we were living and that I was taking good care of her daughter. Two weeks later, Gloria was on our doorstep.

Jackie did begin to model with the world famous Elite Modeling Agency. As usual, I worked hard that off season, increasing the difficulty and duration of my training regimen so that, when the 1986 season opened, I was ready.

———

JOE, ROGER, AND I formed an impressive offensive threesome. Before we ran onto the field prior to games, Roger would say, "You take care of the air, and I'll take care of the ground." And, of course, Joe took control of it all. By the end of the 1986 season, I had amassed 1,570 receiving yards, then the third best season ever by a receiver. But I wasn't as impressive in the playoffs. Early on in a game against the New York Giants, I caught a pass from Joe and headed toward the end zone for a sure touchdown after eluding the Giant's defenders. Then, all of a sudden, I reverted to Jerry the rookie and the ball popped out of my grasp, despite having no one around me, and New York recovered for a touchback. We lost the ball and the momentum and never recovered. When I think back to how I could possibly have fumbled with no one around me, I recall that it was a cold day and I wore long sleeves, which gave me a different arm grip on the ball than if I had been sleeveless. I guess that could have been it but mostly I just think I lost my attention. But I quickly learned to focus. In the next twenty years I had only twenty-four fumbles.

In college, when I could afford a pair, I'd wear receiving gloves, not to help me make catches but because I thought they went well with my uniform—it was all about style. When I first entered the NFL, I wore gloves like many of the receivers in the league but when I started dropping balls in my rookie campaign, I took them off, thinking the gloves were the issue. But I dropped passes even without the gloves. It was then that I realized it wasn't the gloves but my lack of focus that was at the root of the problem. I decided to give the gloves another try and they soon became my security blanket and trademark: white or 49ers maroon, with sticky rubber on the inside, Champion and then Nike, a new pair for every game.

My parents and family back home in Mississippi watched me every week on television, and it meant a lot to me to know that they were there in spirit. Jackie's mother in Greenville would have parties at her home every weekend, as if she was a proud mother—she even let Dallas fans join the celebrations as long as they didn't cheer. Gloria soon had everyone in town rooting for the 49ers; she wore San Francisco jerseys and had 49ers logo stickers on her cars, just in case anyone in town was confused as to her allegiance.

Though I was thrilled to be in San Francisco and had made it out of Mississippi as I had wanted, I never let go of home. I called family and friends all the time and visited at least once a year. I also helped out those back home with financial issues like making a car payment or helping to reduce someone's debt. I felt blessed and was always willing to help, though Jackie routinely told me that I couldn't take care of everyone. I can't save the world but if I can do a small part to help friends and family back home, why not? I never wanted recognition; just a thanks and the satisfaction of knowing I had helped out those in need.

Jackie and I still return to Mississippi every summer, and sometimes we make additional trips during the year. It's important to us to maintain our roots and connection to the state and it is even more important that our kids know where and how we grew up. Despite not always having the fondest memories of home, Mississippi is still home to me and forever will be. But Jackie and I decided to build our own home in the Bay Area many years ago.

Jackie and I had lived together for a year in San Francisco, and things were great between us. Then we got a little surprise—we were pregnant. It was exciting but scary. Jackie was still only nineteen years old at the time. Now that we were going to have a baby, I asked her to marry me—again.

Two months after I had first met Jackie back in Mississippi in

1984, I had asked her for her hand but she had said she was too young. And when I asked her again in 1987, she turned me down for a second time. She didn't want to get married just because she was pregnant. She was confused, and her life was not taking the direction she had planned, having thought all along she would graduate college and become a doctor. She also heard the whispers from the small towns of Mississippi about our life "living in sin" and felt uncomfortable. But after a month or so of thought and, after realizing we were married for all practical purposes anyway, she agreed. I never cared what the whisperers said, and I wasn't going to rush into marriage because of them. But we were ready.

For those of you who are parents, you know the feeling when a child is born. It is miraculous. Our first daughter was born on June 7, 1987, and we named her Jaqui Bonet, after my wife.

I tackled fatherhood as I did everything else in life, with full gusto. The first few weeks Jaqui was home I got up with her in the middle of night, I changed her diapers, I got her dressed, and I did many tasks it seems most fathers leave to mothers. But I loved it. When I was young, like most kids, I planned on getting married and having children of my own when I got older. But when you are the proud parent of your first child, you really start to feel complete as an adult. Here is this little baby who is dependent on you for everything, yet who holds so much promise. I remember soon after Jaqui was born joking with Jackie that it was time for another one!

Gloria came out and helped us with the baby and to plan a wedding celebration, which was slated for September 8, 1987—a Monday. I know, it's not exactly the typical day of the week for a wedding, but then again, I don't work in a typical profession. Almost every week of the football season, we'd play a game Sunday, meet and have a light workout Monday, and then have Tuesday off, so we figured partying Monday night wouldn't interfere with football. The actual ceremony would take place at our house, with just a select few family and friends. Sadly, none of my family members came to the wedding, as they were all terrified of flying (it would be years before my father would even step on a plane), but some of Jackie's family flew out, as they had already been airborne. After the ceremony, we headed over to the Hotel Sofitel in Redwood City where we celebrated with my 49ers teammates and coaches, including Bill Walsh.

For Jackie, being a new mother in a still relatively new city with a budding superstar husband was not easy. She was young, a bit confused, and was adjusting to a brand-new lifestyle. Part of that adjustment included coming to terms with being the wife of a professional athlete. Yes, that meant many days and nights away from home for one's partner, women approaching and propositioning their husbands, drugs, both for recreation and performance, and an assortment of other vices and temptations. There were stories among teammates about players and girlfriends and their trysts on the road (or secretly at home). A prominent professional athlete could be with a different woman every night or indulge in parties and drugs. If I was approached at a bar or a restaurant by a female fan, people would talk and rumors would spread. I am a very approachable guy yet it often fueled speculation about an extramarital love life. (I must admit that the success of *Dancing with the Stars* has opened a whole new can of worms for me with many adoring female fans.) The players' wives talked all the time and they took notice when an "outsider" sat in the family section during games and picked up the phone when they heard stories about possible indiscretions.

For many years, when I got wind of rumors being spread about me, I did what my first instinct told me to do—fight. I would defend myself in the press and seek out those who were spreading rumors, but that's the worst thing I could have done as it just fueled the fire. I soon learned that, ironically, the better I played on the field, the less people cared about what I did—or didn't do—off it.

Despite the advantages of my position, I never let wealth and fame go to my head, never put anything harmful in my body, and kept my focus on football and my family. Roger Craig, Ronnie Lott, and Joe Montana were the same way. I learned from them as they tried to set an example. Just because there are temptations doesn't mean you have to give in to them, and not giving in to them helps you stay humble.

One of the nicest compliments I regularly receive is in regards to my humble demeanor. The assumption seems to be that if you are a star athlete or a celebrity television dancer, you must be arrogant and put yourself above everyone else; but that's simply a generalization. How do I stay humble despite successes? Because I know what it is like on the other side. I know what it's like to grow up poor, to have to prove myself day after day, to play at a small school in Mississippi when many doubted I could ever play in the NFL. My roots have helped me stay humble, even as I broke records in the NFL and won Super Bowls with the 49ers.

Honestly, when I have felt disrespected, I wasn't always the most humble of men, and I made my self-confidence known to reporters who questioned my abilities or voiced concerns over a lack of attention. But being humble means not *needing* the attention and certainly not believing that you are above others. Somehow, humility has found its way out of top tier professional sports. I watch star athletes in football and basketball and baseball gripe about what organizations and owners have not done for them or how they are being misused by their coaches. A real indication of a lack of humility is how athletes carry themselves in public. They get arrested and then claim that they can't be held because they are a star athlete. They insist on over-the-top demands to appear at a charity function. They ignore the fans because they can (those same fans who helped put millions in their pockets). Staying humble is staying true to who you are and treating others with respect, regardless of the level of success that comes your way.

Being famous and wealthy opens up many doors for those lucky enough to live in that world. I see it firsthand. Because of my name and recognition, I can get dinner reservations wherever and whenever I want them. I can get tickets to a sold-out concert. I can get into any nightclub without being on a list or waiting in line. Famous people can get loans from banks that "ordinary" folks could never get. Ironically, I routinely fly low-cost carrier Southwest and enjoy it, much to the surprise of fellow passengers who can't believe I am flying Southwest.

Keep in mind that I am still very shy, and I rarely use my name for anything. In fact, Jackie laughs at me all the time when I choose to stand in line at a club or event rather than cut to the front, though I know I probably can. I'm not going to say, "I'm Jerry Rice, I played for San Francisco and was on *Dancing with the Stars*," to a nightclub bouncer to get in. Okay, I admit it, there is one time of year when I do use the clout my name brings, and that's around Christmas time when it helps me get the latest video games for my kids.

JACKIE AND I HAD our fights like most new couples back in 1987, but believe it or not, perhaps the biggest adjustment for Jackie was coming to terms with my internal drive for perfection. I didn't know any way else to succeed. That's why I put in so many extra hours in the gym or at the practice facility. There was a time when my wife thought I didn't want to be at home spending time with her and Jaqui and we fought about it. But she ultimately acknowledged that it was my drive that kept me away. In our first ten years of marriage, we never traveled. We had the money, but I never took her and Jaqui to a foreign country or a tropical island. We did go to Hawaii for the Pro Bowl week and visited our homes in Mississippi, but we never took advantage of what we could have done, because all I did was eat and sleep football. I regret the time missed with my family but, again, I didn't know any other way. And it would take another nine years before life woke me up.

# Bring It On

THE STRIKE: 1987. We all knew that a players' strike was a real possibility, as the players' union and the team owners had yet to agree on a new contract. Players wanted a form of free agency and better pension benefits and the owners were reluctant to give in on either. As the deadline loomed closer, both sides postured for fan support. Owners began to talk openly in the press about replacement players, and players spoke candidly about the risks of injury, how the physical demands and strain of the sport generally account for short careers in the NFL, and the need for some sort of free agency. At the 49ers complex, we held many player meetings to talk about the issues and to prepare for a strike. Sure enough, it happened, two weeks into the season. We immediately began to picket outside our practice facility and Candlestick Park on game days. We made sure that at least one or two marquee players were visible on the picket lines, as we knew they would attract media attention. We had to make it difficult for the replacement players, whom most of us disliked. How could anyone take someone's job during a strike? I didn't feel bad for the scabs, as we called them; they had invaded our sacred area.

As the games began with replacement players, the owners tried their best to mess with our heads. They were often quoted in the papers talking up some of the replacement players, as if they were good enough to take our spots. I'll be honest, we were all a bit concerned. It was hard not to be. And on Sundays when the games were played, it was even harder to watch. I wanted to be out there. I missed the game so much. I watched the replacement wide receivers with mixed emotions. On the one hand, believe it or not, I wanted them to do well as fellow wide receivers and I enjoyed watching them run great routes and, occasionally, make outstanding catches. On the other hand, I wanted them to fall on their faces to show not only how hard the game was but that there was no way to replace us.

After we missed four games, the strike ended without a new contract and we were eager to get going. But football is about timing and chemistry and it took some time to get it back. Fortunately for us, even non-optimum performances gave us wins.

IN THE MID 1980s, the Cabbage Patch Doll became an international sensation and the toys flew off store shelves. The dolls became so much a part of Americana that a new dance move was named after them, a simple move of raising one's shoulders and pretending to churn butter. I decided before one game that if I scored a touchdown, I'd do a Cabbage Patch dance in the end zone.

And I did. So many players had their celebrations and signature moves and I wanted to put my own stamp on the game. But I was stupid.

On Saturday nights before games, if we had won the previous week, the coaching staff showed us a highlight reel of the best plays from the latest victory. Watching myself celebrate like an ass embarrassed me, though most of my teammates thought it was funny. I didn't need to show off by dancing after scoring. Why not just hand the football to the referee? Joe and Roger were the consummate pros and they didn't need to show off, so why should I? To *be* a professional means to *act* like a professional and, I admit, early on in my career, there were instances when I didn't conduct myself properly. I haven't showboated during a TD celebration since.

A lot has been made of celebrations in recent years, as the NFL has attempted to curb choreographed team dances, skits, and celebrations after touchdowns. There's nothing wrong with a little fun within boundaries, but some of the players today, like Terrell Owens, seem to spend more time planning a celebration than they do concentrating on football. When Owens pulled a Sharpie pen out of his sock to sign the football in a *Monday Night Football* game in 2002 and when he grabbed a cheerleader's pom-poms and danced, I admit, I thought it was funny, but I have to question how much time he devoted to those few seconds in the spotlight. I mean, even during the game he had to be thinking about the pen in his sock and that takes away from the game focus. But T.O.'s celebrations spark debate and that debate creates attention, which is what he craves. Terrell is one of the best, if not *the* best player in the NFL today but his on-field and off-field antics are tarnishing his legacy, which brings me to another point. Doesn't Terrell realize he's a role model to all of the kids watching him?

When I started my career and saw kids wearing my number 80 San Francisco 49ers jersey, it meant something to me and it still does. It meant that I had to do everything I could to set the best example for that young man or woman. Kids come up to me all the time and ask for autographs, and, unless I am with my family trying to have a few minutes alone, I happily oblige. Why? Because if that young boy or girl idolizes me and I don't sign an autograph for him or her, they walk away devastated. They wear my jersey and say they want to be like me, so I'm going to do all I can to set a good example. Some athletes refuse to sign *any* autographs, and some are downright rude to kids. Of course all of this sends the wrong message.

In 1993, basketball star Charles Barkley starred in a Nike commercial, which became quite controversial when Barkley declared that he wasn't a role model just because he was a professional athlete. Charles was right *and* wrong. Pro athletes should never take the place of parents. Parents should be the primary role models for their kids, not some guy they see on television shooting a basketball. But Charles is wrong in not believing that being a role model is part of the job description, whether we like it or not. Professional athletes, and celebrities, are in the spotlight. Being in the spotlight means having millions of impressionable young minds watching our every move. I've been conscious of that ever since I came into the NFL, when I saw the look on kids' faces when they approached me.

A MEMORABLE EVENT during the 1987 season was the game when the term "Hail Jerry" was coined—one of my career highlights. We were on the road in Cincinnati playing the Bengals in Riverfront

Stadium and trailed 26–20 with under a minute to go. As our offense stood on the sideline, we thought the game was over, as Cincy would run out the clock with good game management. Even the 49ers owner, Eddie DeBartolo, Jr., was already walking back to our locker room in disgust. But to our surprise, the Bengals didn't run out the clock as they could have, and we got the ball back with just two seconds remaining on their twenty-five-yard line. As we broke the huddle, Joe pulled me aside and told me if he spotted me in one-on-one coverage, he was going to throw it up there for me to catch. He spotted me in favorable coverage, dropped back to pass, and lofted a perfect throw my way. I jumped as high as I could and came down with the ball.

I remember watching Bill Walsh literally skip across the field with excitement. How was I able to keep calm in that situation? No matter how tense the situation or what is at stake, you need a brief millisecond of distraction. When I lined up on the line of scrimmage as my heart pounded, I'd look into the stands or at a sign or at photographers on the sideline, anything that took me away from the moment at hand. It allowed me to refocus right before the snap so that I had no time to think about what was at stake. Especially for plays after time-outs when I knew well ahead of time the ball was coming my way, I needed a mental break. Professional golfers do the same thing before hitting shots or making million-dollar putts. They take a quick look at the scenery or spectators and then refocus on the next shot.

We finished 1987 with a 13–2 record, but that was a bit misleading since we "regulars" missed a quarter of the season due to the strike. The end result? We lost in the first round of the playoffs to the Minnesota Vikings, though I did finish with an NFL record twenty-two receiving touchdowns.

A sore ankle hobbled me much of 1988. At the start of some games it felt okay, but the injury slowly began to wear on me—as did hits on the field. In an early season game against the New York Giants, I took a lot of cheap shots from their defensive backs, guys like Terry Kinard and Sheldon White, even after I was on the ground. Guys would try to spear me or look to unload on me, even when the ball was on the other side of the field. Anything to hurt me and take me out of the game. And let me tell you, getting hit from the blind side hurts. Bill Walsh always preached composure, so I didn't hit back. I said something to a nearby official and then I told my offensive line what was going on so that the big boys could take care of it. Sure enough, when the Giants started getting some of their own medicine, the cheap shots slowed. All they had left was trash talk and all trash talk did was motivate me.

"You ain't catching anything today!"

"I'm going to break your leg!"

I would get my revenge on players who talked smack not only by sticking it to them in the game, but by taking away their pride and confidence. Just thinking about them painfully watching the game film the next day brought a smile to my face as we won the game. It's all about competition, and I *love* competition.

Sprinters set world records not when they are on the track alone but when they are pushed against top-flight competition. But competition does more than get your juices flowing—it makes you better. When I first got to the 49ers, they already had great wide receivers like Dwight Clark and Freddie Solomon, but I like to think that my arrival pushed all of us to a higher level. The same held true when younger guys like John Taylor, J. J. Stokes, and Terrell Owens entered the fold. Instead of shying away from competition, I embraced it, and it elevated my game. On *Dancing with the*

*Stars,* watching Drew Lachey and Stacy Keibler perform so well in early rounds actually energized me to do better the next time out.

In San Francisco terms, 1988 was mediocre, but we managed to win four of our last five games to win the division title and advance to the playoffs. During the season, quarterbacks Steve Young and Joe Montana both started, creating a headache for Bill Walsh. We beat the Minnesota Vikings 34–9 in our first playoff game, a game in which I scored three touchdowns in the first half. We next faced the Chicago Bears in Chicago in the NFC title game for a shot at the Super Bowl. Now, Candlestick Park in San Francisco can get cold, especially playing at night in late November, but that's nothing compared to the freezing temperatures off Lake Michigan that hit Soldier Field in the dead of winter. Even part of the grass field was frozen solid (which, you'll read, served me well come game time). Some of my teammates and I decided to wear short sleeves on to the field for warm-ups, thinking we were hyped up enough to stay warm. Well, *I* felt the chill. I looked over to the Chicago bench and their players were also in short sleeves, blowing steam in the freezing air, but it didn't seem to bother them. We, however, went back into the locker room and put on long sleeves.

As much as we can try to prepare for the extreme conditions, nothing compares to the reality of a game situation. Coaches routinely have loudspeakers brought into practices blaring crowd noise to try to prepare the team for the noisy stadiums on the road; and they can even bring in fake snow to try to replicate field conditions if white stuff is expected. I guess a coach should have cold air and dry ice brought in to get ready for Chicago.

After the first few offensive plays in the game I realized I had a huge advantage over the defensive players trying to cover me. Because the field was mostly frozen on the outside areas along the sideline, I ran many routes along the boundary because it was hard for them to cut on the frozen field. I knew where I was headed; they didn't. I had two touchdown catches, sixty-one and twenty-seven yarders. We won 28–3 and I had achieved one of my main goals— I was going to play in the Super Bowl. That year, the game was to be played in Joe Robbie Stadium in Miami, Florida, and our opponent was the Cincinnati Bengals. But as we prepared to play the biggest game of our lives, something else took center stage.

# Finally There

**W**E WERE HEADQUARTERED AT the Miami Airport Hilton and Marina, about twenty minutes from downtown Miami, which in the late 1980s was not always a safe place to be, and during this week in mid January 1989, it was really a place to avoid. Race riots had broken out in the Overtown section of Miami County, with looting, fires, and violence, after a Hispanic police officer shot and killed a twenty-three-year-old black man fleeing on a motorcycle, with the resulting crash leading to the death of his passenger the following day. NFL personnel and Miami police had warned us to avoid the area, and even though we were eight miles from the epi-center, it was hard to ignore. The Bengals were at the Omni Hotel, a mere six blocks from the rioting. It was on television, in the news-papers, and it seemed to be all anyone was talking about. I kept watching in disbelief the images on television wondering, *Is this* *real? Is this really happening right now?* Helmeted police officers clashed with rock-throwing youths as looters walked the streets with televisions and groceries. We were in town to play a football game—to entertain fans in Miami and those watching television around the world—yet a few miles away people were getting seriously hurt, even killed. (After three days of riots, two people were dead and twenty-five were injured.)

I hoped that my family was safe, as I had close to eighty friends and family in town for the game. Some had flown in from Mississippi and California, while others drove many hours to see me play, including my mother and father, siblings and friends, all there to share the experience with me. But riots aside, simply accommodating everyone seemed harder than the game might be. I had to take care of eighty tickets, hotel rooms, meals, gas money, and all the details for a very large traveling party. It was mentally exhausting all the way up until game time. And what's more, my right ankle, which I had injured early in the season, was slightly re-aggravated in practice on Monday of Super Bowl week and, despite reports that I was faking the injury, it still wasn't 100 percent by game time. I knew all along that I would play in the game but Bill Walsh threw out the possibility that I might not be ready, to try to throw off Cincinnati, but I don't think they bought it. Everyone knew my work ethic wouldn't stop me from playing. There was also speculation, fueled by some comments by Eddie DeBartolo, that Bill would retire after the game. All-Pro center Randy Cross announced that this would be *his* final game.

Going all the way back to high school, I always had trouble sleeping before games. I was usually so pumped up and anxious that sleeping became a luxury. And in the hours before playing in my first Super Bowl, sleep was nowhere to be found. I was up in the middle of the night, pacing the carpet in my hotel room. My mind was filled with images of the game I was about to play. In practice, the scout team had prepared us well, and I was confident that I knew every defense that might get thrown at me the next day. So in my mind I took myself onto the field, watching as the plays developed, visualizing making catches and scoring touchdowns. I never thought of us winning, just me making the plays. Staying up thinking about the game in this fashion goes against my theory of never wasting energy, but that theory gave way to "Whatever works, do it!"

The next day (really, one long day that covered a night) I headed over to the stadium early, as I typically did before games. I put on my pants and jersey to prepare for warm-ups and quickly took a seat on a nearby table. The next thing I knew, I fell asleep right there in the middle of the locker room, snoring away! Just hours before the biggest game of my life I'm taking a nap. I awoke to the sounds of my teammates talking as they passed by and we finally took the field. The ensuing moments were unforgettable—not only the thousands of fans on hand, but the fireworks, the smoke, the media crush. For me, it was heaven. There were only two teams playing that day and the world was watching.

Keep in mind that though we were a good football team, we hadn't been as dominating during the regular season as we had been in the past, so there was some extra confidence on the Cincinnati sideline. The field at Joe Robbie Stadium had been sodded five weeks prior to the game, but that didn't stop chunks of midfield from popping up early.

Things didn't start off well for us. On the third play of the game, big left tackle Steve Wallace broke his left ankle, which left a gaping hole in our offensive line. The game started out low-scoring (tied at halftime 3–3), but after the break the points started to rain. On a third quarter kickoff, the Bengals' Stanford Jennings returned the kick ninety-three yards for the game's first touchdown, and suddenly we found ourselves trailing 13–6 as the third quarter came to a close. We started our drive on our own fifteen-yard line but with some great running and receiving by Roger Craig, great passing by Joe Montana, and a few catches by John Taylor and me, we worked our way down to the Bengals' fourteen-yard line. I lined up in the slot position, caught a pass from Joe at the five-yard line, and worked my way into the end zone for a touchdown, tying the game at 13.

Cincinnati responded with a good drive of its own, converting a field goal, to take a 16–13 lead with just 3:10 left in the game. Then, a penalty on us on the kickoff backed us up to our own eight-yard line. It would all come down to the last minutes of the fourth quarter. With 190 seconds to go, we started the drive ninety-two yards from the end zone. In that situation, there was no one you wanted at quarterback more than Joe Montana. He was typically calm, while calling out two plays in every huddle, while squatting down and picking grass. When we broke that first huddle, for me, everything went completely quiet. I was in such a zone I could hear nothing but Joe's plays. Afterward, some of the guys talked about the now famous offhanded comment that Joe allegedly made to offensive lineman Harris Barton in the huddle, "Hey, isn't that John Candy?" (This story gets told repeatedly because it shows how cool Joe was in that type of pressure situation.) I honestly can't confirm or deny that comment because I was so focused on moving the ball ninety-two yards with limited time that any extraneous comments would've been lost on me. It's hard to articulate that sort of competitive state. You frequently hear Michael

Jordan talk about being "in the zone," and I can only assume that his definition and mine are the same—it's crunch time, your concentration is at its peak, and your only objective is to make plays to get your team into a position to win. Your mind rejects any and all distractions. Passes to Roger, tight end John Frank, and to me helped move us downfield in a hurry. I knew we would score. One day of every week of the season, we would run the "two-minute drill," simulating a drive with little time remaining on the clock. We would run it at the end of practice, when we were tired, as if it were a game situation. We always took the drill seriously and we always executed it well in practice, so I was confident the Super Bowl finish would yield a similar result.

On the ninth play of the drive, we faced a second and ten on the Bengals' thirty-five-yard line. Our big center, Randy Cross, was penalized for illegally being downfield after Roger made a catch and we were backed up to the forty-five-yard line and now faced a second and twenty. I ran a square in route across the middle and beat three defenders—Lewis Billups, Roy Horton, and David Fulcher—to the ball, and somehow eluded all of them after the catch, taking the ball another fourteen yards for a twenty-seven-yard gain and a first down. An eight-yard pass to Roger set up a second and two on Cincy's ten-yard line. Then fate took over.

Now everyone on the field and in the stands thought the ball was coming my way. I had three catches on the drive and history had shown that Montana and Rice were the go-to guys in the clutch. But Bill Walsh recognized that, and called for a play in which I would be a decoy, not the main target. The play was called "20 Halfback Curl X Up" with Roger Craig as the primary receiver and John Taylor as the read receiver. I went into motion, running from one side of the field to the other before the snap, serving as a decoy. Joe dropped back, Roger was jammed and covered, but he spotted John Taylor in favorable coverage, and hit him in stride for a touchdown. At that moment, the silence turned into deafening cheers. I felt like I had made the catch. Sometimes for the good of the team, you have to "suck it up" and be unselfish. I was just thrilled that we had scored. We led 20–16 with just thirty-four seconds to go and held on for the Super Bowl victory. In the last drive, Joe completed eight of nine passes for ninety-seven yards (penalty yards included) and finished with 357 yards for the day. I finished with eleven catches for 215 yards and a touchdown, and I was named Super Bowl Most Valuable Player.

But in the ensuing days, I found myself in the middle of a media firestorm. After the game, it was Joe, not I, who uttered the familiar phrase, "I'm going to Disney World!" into the cameras. It was the first time a non–Super Bowl MVP had been the face of the famous Disney commercial, and it wouldn't happen again for another six years. It upset me. In addition to that slight, much of the media attention after the game was on Joe and Bill Walsh. On San Francisco television station KRON, I said the following: "If it was Joe Montana or Dwight Clark [winning MVP] it would be headlines all over. I'm not the type that wants . . . all the recognition, but I felt like I deserved to get some of it."

In what I still believe was an overblown situation, the media reported that I was unhappy with my lack of attention and publicity after being awarded the MVP, and that I had implied that race had something to do with it. Some writers blamed my comments on the lack of endorsements that came my way, though that wasn't true. But there was racism in the San Francisco Bay Area, just like there was back home in Mississippi. It was there, just below the surface. I was a black athlete and many of us had seen subtle racism take hold. I should have been more careful with my words but I don't regret making the point. If a white superstar had been the Super Bowl MVP, things would have been different, with more attention from the media and fans.

In 2003, commentator Rush Limbaugh made controversial comments on ESPN while talking about the Philadelphia Eagles' black quarterback Donovan McNabb, declaring that McNabb was overrated by an agenda-driven media wanting a black quarterback to be successful. In the not so distant past, black quarterbacks were forced to play other positions because coaches didn't think they could get it done behind center; that they didn't have the intelligence to play quarterback. And there are barely any black coaches to start with. But simply being a black athlete, I have always felt I've had to prove myself and be very successful just to be accepted.

There was other news going on after the Super Bowl, including speculation about Joe Montana's future with the 49ers, but then the bombshell hit: Bill Walsh was really stepping down. Bill was asked in the postgame press conference if he had coached his last game. His comments were vague and elusive but shortly thereafter Bill did indeed retire, replaced by defensive coordinator George Seifert. It hurt me tremendously to see Bill move on. I had laid it all on the line for him every day. I would have run through a brick wall for that man. He was the one who gave me the opportunity with the 49ers and he was my west coast father. I was confident that George could do a good job since Bill had recommended him and I trusted Bill's judgment completely, but since George had always worked with the defense, I didn't know him that well.

THE OFF-SEASON WORKOUTS continued and in the beginning of May, I began training with Raymond Ferris and Roger Craig and a few other guys in San Carlos, south of San Francisco. There was a track we could use and some great running hills, not to mention beautiful scenery. Almost daily, we met for grueling workouts at seven thirty a.m. Three times a week we would run up a two-and-a-half-mile hill, running against the clock. The last eight hundred yards was a steep incline to the finish. It is a real gut check when you are a half mile out. If you couldn't endure the pain, if you couldn't see yourself at the top level in the fourth quarter, the hill wasn't for you. I was in such good condition from running the hill that during the season, there was little difference in my play from the start of the game until the final whistle.

On the days we didn't run the hill, we worked on speed at a track, mixing in short-distance runs and sprints. We would run eight two-hundred-meter sprints, followed by ten one-hundred-meter sprints. Then we would do a lot of cone drills, sprinting forward, backward, and laterally—all under the hot summer sun. And after all of our conditioning workouts, be it on the hill or the track, I headed to the gym to lift weights for another two and a half hours, three days working on my upper body, three days on the lower body.

Every off season, we ran the same program in San Carlos and word quickly spread. Our 49ers teammates soon joined us, as did friends from other teams who wanted to be in top shape for the season. On average, there might be fifteen of us training on a given day, peaking our training in late June, right before camp would open. Some of the participants included J. J. Stokes, Ricky Waters, Barry Sanders, Steve Bono, Roger Craig, Tom Rathman, and a few guys who showed up for a day but decided it wasn't for them. But not everyone worked hard in the off season. Some guys did absolutely nothing and waited until training camp to get into shape. My 49ers teammate John Taylor was like that; he did nothing in the off season but still somehow managed to be great. Some guys did a little bit of running in late June but it took them until the regular season was under way before getting into game shape. All of that hard work earned us the extra yard after a catch, the extra breath on the field, the one-second more of burst we needed.

BACK IN THE MID 1980s, when I first entered the NFL, anabolic steroids began to become popular. Steroids were muscle enhancement drugs that helped athletes get bigger and stronger quickly. I never saw anyone take steroids and never knew for sure if any player did. While I was playing, the former Raider great Lyle Alzado died of brain cancer in 1992, brought on by his admitted use of steroids while playing in the league. Players who take steroids are only doing their bodies harm. For what? A few extra years in a career that may mean less years of life? As athletes, we know exactly what we are putting into our bodies, which is why I had to smirk when I read that Barry Bonds made statements that he didn't know what his trainers were giving him in response to steroid-use allegations related to the now-infamous BALCO investigation. C'mon, he knew exactly what he was doing.

Why does steroid use bother me so much? For one thing, it is totally unfair to those of us who play the game clean and puts us at an unfair disadvantage. I'm old school. If you want to get better, put in the hard work and sweat. There is no substitute for hard work. It's one of the reasons I am a big proponent of drug testing throughout the NFL, for steroids and for all other drugs. You have to have a tough drug testing policy to keep the game as clean as possible. Random testing, which the league has now, is the best method, as players have just twenty-four hours to take the test once their names show up.

IN THE SUCCEEDING TWO years under George Seifert, 1989 and 1990, we went 14–2 in each of the regular seasons, with the '89 season culminating in another Super Bowl victory, this one over the Denver Broncos in a whitewash, 55–10. The Broncos defensive players had been talking smack in the media before the game, saying they'd punish me with vicious hits. I had seven catches for 148 yards and three touchdowns. Joe Montana was named the game's MVP, in a vote that could have gone either way.

In 1990, against Atlanta in mid-October, I scored five touchdowns and caught thirteen passes and we once again had a great regular season, but a few breakdowns on defense cost us during the playoffs, and we lost to the New York Giants in the NFC title game.

The Giants were then coached by Bill Parcells, who many consider among the greatest coaches. He may be, but his confrontational style and the way he treats players have kept some players away, even today with the Dallas Cowboys. Bill is always upfront, sometimes too upfront with his players, from what they tell me. Still, they know exactly where they stand. He likes to test guys, to see how much they can endure and he likes the "nasty" guys who find ways to get it done, so he and new Cowboy Terrell Owens are a perfect fit.

Joe Montana was everything to our football team and to the San Francisco organization, so when he injured his elbow in the NFC title game against the Giants, we were all devastated. He kept the team together in tough times and led us to the promised land, so when the mighty Joe injured his elbow, it seemed like the world was caving in. Joe and I had such great chemistry on the field; we just knew what each other was thinking and what we needed to do to make the other's job easier.

Bill Walsh always used to tell the team that when you get an opportunity, you have to take advantage of it, and that's exactly what an eager Steve Young did. I was quite skeptical, to be honest, when Steve stepped into the starting quarterback role. First of all, he was left-handed, meaning everything would change for me, as I had never caught passes from a lefty in my life. Second, in practice, Steve had earned a reputation as a running quarterback, meaning that he wasn't afraid to take off running if he didn't spot any open receivers. Again, a big change for me and the other wide receivers. All receivers want the ball thrown their way and anything that may reduce the number of balls thrown to them is not viewed as a good thing.

I've always been open to criticism and I always felt that I was coachable and flexible. I'm not afraid to change if it will make me better. With "Uncle Steve," as I called him, replacing Joe, I had no choice. Everything that Joe and I had was placed on the back burner. To adjust to catching from a left-handed quarterback, I spent hours on the practice field catching balls thrown by our equipment manager, Ted Walsh, who happened to be a lefty. Now, he wasn't an NFL QB but I got used to seeing the ball come from the other arm. With a lefty, the ball comes out of the hand with a reverse spin that I wasn't used to—the ball spins to the left. When the ball met the palms of my hands, it just felt different.

After adjusting to throws from a lefty, I also had to adjust my routes and the way I got open. You see, Steve was a running quarterback and that meant if I didn't get open quickly, he would tuck the ball under his arm and take off himself. Joe was more patient in the pocket, allowing us more time to get free. Over the course of my career, I caught passes from a variety of quarterbacks and I always tried to adjust to them, never getting to a complacent point. Joe didn't have the strongest arm and he released the ball early, almost lofting it; Steve had a bullet arm and could drill the ball like John Elway or Brett Favre; Rich Gannon threw sidearm and his release point made it tough to judge the ball.

Suffice it to say, Steve and I went on to become a very productive tandem in the NFL. Actually, we would end up connecting on more touchdown passes than Joe and I did. But to this day, fans constantly ask me about Joe and Steve. Who was the better quarterback? Who did I like connecting with? It was Joe. There was just something special about the way he carried himself, his leadership, and his abilities as a quarterback. Taking nothing away from Steve, of course, who proved that he is among the NFL's best, but if I had a choice of quarterbacks to be behind center in a big game, there was no question it would be Joe.

ON THE FIELD, 1991 was a unique year. Not only was Joe out with an injury but two of my favorite teammates and tremendous players, Roger Craig and Ronnie Lott, had left the 49ers for the Los Angeles Raiders before the season. The 49ers were headed in a new direction. George Seifert wanted his own guys to start something new. So after Joe went down, there was no Joe, Roger, or Ronnie. Quite simply, this was a team and an organization in transition. I was the "last of the Mohicans"; the sole remaining star player from the dynasty of the 1980s. I understood that the NFL was a business, but I was still sad not to have those guys on my side. They were the rock of the only NFL team I had been on. I knew I had to take the weight onto my shoulders, to be more vocal in the absence of leadership. There were times in team meetings or in pregame talks or during emotional halftimes when I stood before my teammates to give encouragement or to blast a lack of effort. The guys needed to hear me and I believed that I had earned their respect through years of hard work and success. If I gave some Vince Lombardi/Knute Rockne pep talk before every game, my words would have gotten lost, as players can only hear from you so many times. I had to pick my moments when to stand up and choose my words carefully.

The season started out poorly, not only because Joe was out, but because I injured my right knee in the second game of the season. An MRI revealed that I had torn the posterior cruciate ligament (PCL). Fortunately, with some great 49ers trainers, I didn't have to sit out any games. The injury wasn't as severe as it could have been and, again, I learned to adjust. I taught myself how to cut and turn without putting full pressure on the right knee. Repetitions in practice retrained my muscles and I learned how to step without pain. Though my technique and a few of my routes had changed, I never sensed a drop-off in my productivity, finishing the 1991 season with eighty catches and 1,206 yards. But we started off 2–4 on the year, and things never really got right.

As I adapted to the new signal-caller on the football field, I also adapted to a larger family at home. The Rice family expanded in the summer of 1991 as little Jerry Jr. was born during the middle of training camp in late July. It had been four years since Jaqui was born, and I did all the fatherly tasks once again, changing diapers, getting up in the middle of the night, etc. Having a son made me think a lot more about my own relationship with my father. I would be a role model for Jerry Jr. and prepare him for life as my father had done for me, but I would try to do it without the fear.

We were a family in transition and a football organization in flux. Was it time to let go of the past or would loyalty reign supreme? My own stupidity and selfishness wouldn't make the choice any easier.

# Nothing Lasts Forever

**H**OW YOU PRACTICE = How you play.

It's that simple. I don't care if we're talking about basketball or ballet, cooking or checkers. The way in which you prepare for a challenge is usually related to your success in that same challenge. If the level at which you practice is commensurate with the task, then on "game day," you'll be fine.

When I first joined the San Francisco 49ers, I brought with me something that I had adopted early on in my football career: running out every catch in practice. So even after the most simple receiving route and catch, I would go full speed toward the end zone. I know many of the veterans thought I was crazy, or that I was a hot dog trying to show them up, but it's the only way I know how to practice—to treat it like a game. Sure enough, some of my teammates took my lead and before long we were all running out every play in practice. That's not a testament to me, but an ode to practicing the way you want to play.

San Francisco had something else during my time there: veterans willing to lead. Veterans like Freddie Solomon and Dwight Clark and Roger Craig set the example for the rookies. So many young superstars in football and basketball today come in with so much money and so few examples to follow. Allen Iverson is an All-Star basketball player who never took a liking to practice but then again, who did he have to teach him hard work?

John Taylor, my former teammate with the 49ers, was not always the best practice player. He never seemed to want to practice. Most of the time, he didn't even stretch. But he could jump and he could play football. He was a good player, and I depended on him a lot to make catches when I was double-teamed. But John and I clearly had a different view on preparation. I could never understand how someone couldn't find the motivation to push himself in practice. John is the extreme example of someone who could perform without real practice. Just imagine how much better he could have been had he believed in Practice = Play. He could have been great; instead, he was just good.

Training camp started in July 1992, but for the first time ever, I didn't show up for practice. Despite my love for the game and my teammates, football is still a business at its core, as the 49ers vets had reminded me years ago. My agent and I believed it was in my best interest to hold out from 49ers camp in order to send a message to the organization that we needed a better contract. I had proven my value to the team and wanted to be compensated as such. At the time, and still today, agents advise their clients to hold out to force the owner's hand. (Even though this was contrary to my parents' lesson that money isn't everything, it is in the business of football.) Though you may hear about six- or seven-year contracts in the NFL, the reality is that none of those years are guaranteed. That is, you can be cut at any time, and the organization does not have to pay you for the remaining years on the contract. To that end, most long-term contracts are heavy on the back end, meaning the huge salary and bonuses don't kick in until the later years of the deal, when it's often to the benefit of the team to let you go or trade you. That is why you may read now about the huge signing bonuses that draft picks demand. Since the contract money is not guaranteed but the signing bonus is, it's well worth it to get as much up front as possible.

So in 1992, I stayed away from training camp—and, to that point, it was the worst time of my life. I hated every day that I wasn't out there with my teammates. I trained hard on my own but it wasn't the same. I didn't feel connected, and I even felt disloyal in some ways. We were able to work out a deal and I finally returned to camp, but I felt as if I was behind. It took some practice days to get back into the flow. The way you practice is the way you play, and missing that practice time would cost us. I can tell you now that I made a huge mistake and regret holding out. It's better to be in camp and show your loyalty by working toward the start of the season as a team than to refuse to practice to prove a point. I try to tell the younger guys in the league what I learned but, sadly, many are all about the money and their agents get their way.

THE 1992 SEASON TURNED out better than 1991, but it still wasn't great. Joe Montana continued to rehab his elbow and missed much of 1992, but he did get to the point where he could re-enter the starting lineup. Despite the fact that Steve Young had developed into a very good quarterback in 1991 and 1992, I felt it was Joe's job to lose and I made a few public comments to that end, which I am sure the front office personnel and coaching staff did not appreciate. Joe had meant so much to the organization and had shown such loyalty that I only thought they should return the loyalty. (And remember, I thought Joe was the better quarterback.) Joe did get a start in a late-season Monday night game against the Detroit Lions, but Steve had a great season as our full-time QB, leading us to fourteen wins and, despite a loss to Dallas in the NFC championship game, he earned NFL MVP honors. As a result, I knew this was Joe's last season in a 49ers uniform. Whether or not he continued his career with another team would be up to him.

There was a minor, however scary, hiccup along the way for me in the 1992 season—the result of a rookie mistake. "The Genius" Walsh had always reminded his receivers not to "dance." That is, after catching a ball, make a quick move and then head upfield, don't get fancy, a rule that I routinely followed. In the NFL, many injuries to wide receivers don't happen in trying to catch the ball but in trying to eke out a few more yards after the catch. And against Buffalo, I danced. After making a catch, I tried to be a bit too fancy with my footwork and earn the extra yards, and the defense was just looking to take my head off. Defensive players, particularly the huge linemen, are taught to take off running downfield the moment the ball is released from the quarterback's hand. Well, the Bills' linemen, most of whom weighed well above three hundred pounds, did just that and as I danced, they attacked. The next thing I remember, I was on the sideline with trainers.

Apparently, I had been knocked out on the field. Clocked cold. My teammates said they heard me snoring and saw drool rolling down the side of my mouth. On the bench, trainers asked me what

I had had for breakfast and what day of the week it was, trying to determine just how bad the concussion was. They told me if I went back in, there could be real damage, so I agreed to sit this one out.

In 1993, we went 10–6 and made it to the title game. The previous season, we had lost the title game at home to Dallas, and in '93, it was all about pride. I stood before my teammates and pleaded with them that if we had any pride at all, we had to win. We couldn't lose to the hated Cowboys again. We lost anyway, 38–21. I wasn't proud of the way we played and I certainly wasn't proud that we had lost two years in a row with a Super Bowl berth on the line. (We finally beat them the next season at home.)

After we lost to Dallas, rumors and reports began to swirl that I was considering retirement. It didn't make sense. I was relatively injury-free and I had just come off the 1993 season with over fifteen hundred yards receiving and fifteen touchdowns. Ah, but once again, the business of football reared its ugly head. And in the vicious business of the NFL, rumors that make it to print often have an agenda behind them, especially when it concerns guys like me who have been around a while. Much of the speculation gets started by coaches or organizational personnel or agents with an agenda.

Let's say, for example, that the 49ers don't want to pay me a certain amount of money, though they know I deserve it. A few assistant coaches or front office people begin to be "anonymously" quoted in the papers as saying I'm thinking about retirement, even though I had never given it one thought. Floating the idea allows the organization to see what media and fan reaction would be. Soon, the media runs with it and begins to ask me questions and before I know it, I'm thinking maybe I should consider retiring! I still enjoyed practice, my heart was in it, and I was healthy and productive. Why should I stop playing? I didn't but I had a hunch there were those in the 49ers organization who had started the rumors—and I didn't like it.

As for Joe, 1992 was the end of the line for him with the San Francisco organization. In April 1993, the trade happened so fast, none of us had time to react. It was like the Baltimore Colts moving to Indianapolis in the middle of the night. Joe was off to Kansas City. I never got the chance to say good-bye and Joe never had a chance to address his teammates. I regret not being more vocal to 49ers management and in the media about Joe's departure. He was the San Francisco 49ers and should have been treated better. I know that Steve Young had developed into a great QB at the time, but at the very least, the 49ers should have treated Joe with class.

# Prime Time

**I** REPORTED TO TRAINING camp the next summer two days before the other veterans to work out with the rookies and free agents to get a start on the season. There was another money issue in training camp in 1994, but this one didn't concern me. The team was going to cut loose two players on the practice squad, as they didn't want to pay for their salaries. Now, for those of you who have never played football, the practice or scout players are invaluable. They are the ones who study an upcoming opponent to mimic their tendencies and play against the starters in practice to prepare us for game days. Scout team players have helped me immensely over the years.

There were two guys in particular that year whom I had watched and thought had a chance to move up to roster spots and help the team down the road. I didn't want to see them released because of salary issues. I had been very fortunate in my career and wanted to give a little back, so I offered $170,000 of money that I would have earned through incentives to pay the salary of the two guys. Only a few people inside the organization knew about the gesture and I wanted it that way. But the 49ers thought of the goodwill of publicity that would surely come their way and word trickled out to the media. I was proud of what I had done but embarrassed by the praise. The most gratifying praise I could ever have received was when the two players approached me and thanked me. That was enough.

Jackie and I always felt blessed with the financial rewards that came with my NFL career and we did whatever we could to make the lives of our loved ones better. In addition to building my parents the house back in the mid-1980s, we bought Gloria a home in Greenville. Occasionally, we have splurged on ourselves, buying a Porsche and some fancy jewelry and nice clothing here and there. But despite our blessed wealth, we've always made sure to raise our children to value money and to be role models. We have given to a variety of causes, whether it's a church in Mississippi or cancer causes. Later, we would establish the 127 Foundation to more formally consolidate our charity work. We held golf tournaments every year to raise money for the foundation and much of the proceeds went to the March of Dimes or Big Brothers/Big Sisters.

THE YEAR 1994 MARKED the arrival of "Prime Time" in San Francisco. Deion Sanders was a great football player who had most recently played for the Atlanta Falcons. He was a tremendous defensive back, able to shut down top receivers in one-on-one coverage, and also contributed as a kick and punt returner for Atlanta (but he wouldn't take on those roles in San Francisco). When Deion touched the ball, he electrified the crowd. But Deion also brought a huge posse with him wherever he went. He brought a carefree attitude and showmanship beyond anything I could have imagined. He was more about entertaining than playing football. I was concerned about what his attitude and flash might mean to the 49ers. Like most teams, the organization talked to some of us veterans about all potential signings, including that of Deion. I was skeptical, but I also knew we needed him to get us back to Super Bowl caliber.

Deion and I respected each other but we had waged battles over our years in the NFL. I remember one game against Atlanta when Deion played for them in which he tried to shake my hand after we broke the huddle on the first play of the game while our QB was calling out signals. Maybe he was trying to get into my head, but Deion should have known better—this was battle. I had some success playing against him, though it certainly took more effort on my part than was typical. You see, Deion is so fast off the line of scrimmage that I had to do a double or triple move after the ball was snapped to try to get by him. We had engaged in so many battles that I doubted we could ever be friends.

Our first game of the 1994 season was against the rival Los Angeles Raiders on *Monday Night Football.* Playing on Monday night always got me fired up, but to add to my usual excitement, I was two touchdowns shy of tying the legendary Jim Brown for the NFL touchdown record of 126. No one, including me, believed that I would tie him, much less break the record, in the first game of the season, as scoring three TDs is a lot to ask in one game, let alone the opener. I scored my first touchdown off a post route early in the game to close to within one of tying Brown. I scored a second touchdown on a reverse play to tie the record. Everyone in the stadium knew where I stood and I appreciated the ovation for tying the mark. But could I actually break the record?

We pulled away in the game and led 37–14 with just over four minutes remaining and typically George Seifert was not one to run up the score. But on this night, he pulled me aside very late in the second half to tell me he would give me one opportunity to break the record, so I could do it in front of the home crowd. One play, one pass, to get it done on *Monday Night Football.* As I ran onto the field, everyone stood and held their breath with anticipation. They knew what was coming, I knew what was coming, the Raiders defenders knew what was coming, and so did the Raiders' flamboyant owner, Al Davis.

I jogged onto the field and listened as Steve Young called the play. I went into motion to the left side and then sprinted downfield. Bill Walsh had always taught receivers that the best way to catch a ball was at its highest point—to jump and snare it before it begins to descend. So when I saw the ball headed my way, I leaped as high as I could and attacked the football. I fought off defender Albert Lewis, beating him by inches to the ball, and scored the record-breaking touchdown. I was so focused on the ball I didn't even hear the crowd until after I stood up in the end zone. My teammates swarmed me and picked me up on the field.

In the postgame locker room interviews, I credited my teammates and, though honored by the record and the comparisons to Jim Brown, I still was not impressed with myself. In fact, later that night, back at home, I did what I always did after a game—played it back in my mind. I thought about what I did well on certain plays and what I could have done better on others. The next day, I was at the practice facility a few hours before the rest of the crew, working out. I never paused to admire what I had done.

As for Deion, he lived up to the hype, on and off the field. He shut down opponents and gave our defense a much-needed spike in enthusiasm, intercepting six passes and scoring three touchdowns that season. Away from the field, he was all Prime Time, wearing fancy clothes and jewelry, traveling with a large posse and often hosting parties, going out to L.A. parties and San Francisco nightclubs, and talking, talking, talking. We rolled through the season and overcame our nemesis in the NFC championship game, finally beating Dallas to get back to the Super Bowl, where we would face San Diego. This would be my third Super Bowl so I knew what to expect: the routine, the media, the distractions. The practice week was going well until a group of players missed curfew, enjoying the nightlife a little too much. In a full team meeting, I picked my moment and rose to speak. Addressing all of the players who missed curfew the previous night, including Deion Sanders, I implored them to focus on the task at hand.

"You can party anytime, all during the year, but not now," I told them. "Heck, I'll even party with you when it's all over. But we are preparing for the biggest game in our careers." I was mad. Angry at those who had sacrificed our chances of winning for a late night of partying. It wasn't just Prime Time, it was all the guilty parties. As a team, we had a shared responsibility. "Nobody remembers the loser of the Super Bowl," I reminded the team. I talked for maybe seven or eight minutes and, admittedly, let loose a few curse words. It was enough.

After word leaked out to the media about my comments to the team, the media made it all about Jerry versus Deion to sell papers, though that wasn't the case. Saturday night, the night before the game, everyone made curfew.

On the day of the Super Bowl, we put the missed curfews behind us as we took the field against the underdog Chargers. Just over a minute into the game, Steve Young and I connected on a forty-four-yard touchdown pass play. In the second quarter, however, I got a little too caught up in the moment and made a stupid decision. On a reverse play, I took the ball and headed out toward the sideline to find some room. When the gap closed quickly, the smart thing to do, the thing we are taught to do, is to simply run out of bounds and move on to the next play. But not me. I once again had to go for the extra yards, challenging a defensive back to stop me. The result: a separated shoulder.

The trainers took me back to the locker room and told me I had a third grade dislocation. They gave me shots of cortisone, supposedly to help ease the pain. I don't know what they had in the syringe, but it certainly didn't help. I told them to tape it up and I would find a way through it. I returned to the sideline and the game, scoring two touchdowns in the second half after the injury. (It's important to note here that if I thought I could do real damage to myself or that my being on the field at less than 100 percent would hurt the team, I never would have returned. In this case, the doctors left it up to me.) We went on to blow out the Chargers, 49–26, and won our third Super Bowl.

Remember how I told you that I was disappointed back in 1985? That though I was named Rookie of the Year I wasn't selected for the Pro Bowl in Hawaii? Well, every time I was picked for the Pro Bowl I made it a priority to go there and play hard, as opposed to some players who didn't care about practice or the game and just enjoyed the beach life and the parties. Even though I had the separated shoulder from the Super Bowl, I still flew to Hawaii and practiced and ran routes hard. That's just who I am.

After the 1994 season and the Super Bowl victory, Prime Time moved on and signed with Dallas, after a very protracted and public courtship. But it seemed the media couldn't let go of Deion. After we beat his former team, the Atlanta Falcons, 41–10, in 1995, reporters kept asking about Deion and what his departure meant for us. The 49ers were not, and never were, about Deion. We still had many bright stars on our team and for some reason I exploded. I unleashed some curse words in the locker room directed at the reporters. "It's an insult to the guys who were busting their butts!" I screamed, referring to criticism in the press that the 49ers defense was worse without Deion. I regret exploding but I stand by my point.

AH, REPORTERS. They come in all shapes and sizes. As in any profession, there are good ones and bad ones. Newspapers had always dominated the NFL beat but soon talk radio became a major player and, later, the millions of Web sites devoted to teams, mostly filled with gossip. After my initial surprise at the media crunch when I landed in San Francisco in 1985, nothing surprised me when it came to the press. I tried to be as accommodating and professional as possible (which didn't always happen). Jackie has always supported me when it came to the media and, though she and I will admit I could have phrased things a bit differently, I always spoke from the heart. There were times that things were written about me or said about me on the radio that simply weren't true. Quotes from me were taken out of context or simply quoted incorrectly. Occasionally, when that happened, I chose to confront the reporter on the inaccuracies or items I thought were unfair. One reporter, Glenn Dickey of the *San Francisco Chronicle,* wrote a particularly irksome column in 1998, after an injury had slowed me down the previous season. Glenn pointed out that Steve Young was still trying to run an offense through me though I wasn't at my best anymore. Well, not only didn't I like the swipe at me, but also at Steve. Coming off the practice field one day I yelled at Glenn. A week later, I spotted him in the locker room and offered an apology.

I always tried to talk to reporters in private, but it didn't always happen that way. I would call them out in front of their peers on issues I felt strongly about. But that was probably the wrong approach since all it did was give attention to an attention-starved reporter.

Glenn and Ira Miller, also from the *San Francisco Chronicle*, were critical of my being drafted by the team back in 1985, and their criticism of me never let up. They jumped on me in the newspapers when I dropped a pass and ignored the touchdowns and hard work. I think they never really liked the whole 49ers organization and I don't know why. But toward the end of my stay in San Francisco, the relationship between us improved. I think Glenn and Ira respected my loyalty and hard work over the years and they slowly changed their tunes.

Athletes read the papers, listen to talk radio, and watch television, so don't let them fool you. They know what is being said and written about them and they know who said it and who wrote it. I was one of those guys who read every word and often, as I mentioned earlier, I used columns and articles as motivation. I know. I shouldn't have to rely on reading something in a newspaper to get me fired up but I've always found external motivations in my career. I made a huge mistake in 1993 after seething over what I perceived as slights in Glenn and Ira's stories. I decided to stop talking to the media for two weeks, acting like an immature child. At the time, I thought I was doing the right thing, to prove a point. I was wrong. It unfairly punished other members of the press who had done nothing wrong (as reporters and 49ers public relations staff pointed out to me) and it didn't help the situation. The worst thing you can do is shut out the media because it simply gives them more reasons to write negative stories.

THE MEDIA WASN'T TOO positive in 1995 since we didn't make it back to the Super Bowl. I finished with 122 catches and 1,848 receiving yards and, along the way, became the NFL all-time leader in receptions, breaking James Lofton's record in late October. It was one of my best years but Brett Favre was voted the NFL MVP that year over me.

But who won the MVP Award in 1995 paled in comparison to what happened next in my life.

# Feeling the Faith

JAQUI AND JERRY JR. were wonderful kids who brought so much joy into our lives, so when we found out we were pregnant with a third child in late 1995, we couldn't have been happier. Jackie was due in May of 1996, which would be perfect timing with football training camp not getting under way until July. As was the case during the previous two pregnancies, Jackie's mother, Gloria, flew out from Mississippi before the birth to lend support and a helping hand. When Jackie went into labor on May 16 in Mills Hospital in nearby San Mateo, I stood in the delivery room for the third time, and my mother-in-law was right there with us. She sat at the foot of the bed watching the actual birth while I stood near Jackie's head, holding her hand and lending her encouragement. (Gloria joked that if I had seen the actual birth I would have fainted. Maybe. I certainly don't like needles and blood and bones. I haven't even been able to bring myself to watch Joe Theismann's horrendous broken leg injury against the New York Giants from 1985.) When Jackie delivered Jaqui and Jerry Jr., labor went quickly, and it was the same when little Jada Rice was born. Everything went perfectly with the delivery and we had a beautiful baby girl.

After I cut the umbilical cord, Dr. Andrew Jurow began to try to ease out the placenta from Jackie. But five minutes later, he still couldn't remove it from her and she was bleeding heavily. Suddenly, Dr. Jurow had a scared look on his face and I could tell something was wrong. Things happened so quickly after that. While Jada was being groomed for her new world and put into the nursery, Jackie was about to undergo what we believed was a routine procedure. I told her I loved her as they wheeled her hospital bed directly into the operating room.

At three p.m., when Jackie was taken into surgery, the hospital was undergoing a daily shift change, when nurses from the early shift and night shift trade places. There was one nurse in particular who had been with us throughout the day; she refused to go home until after Jackie came out of surgery and she knew she was all right. So as the doctors worked on Jackie, Gloria, the kids (whom our housekeeper had picked up from school), and I laid around the hospital waiting room, anticipating the doctor's favorable report, eager to spend time with Jackie and the new baby. But the wait grew longer as the afternoon became night. And each time we asked a nurse about her condition, she would tell us we could see Jackie in twenty minutes. Soon, the minutes had turned into hours. As you might imagine, my concern grew. She was the love of my life and I was helpless.

At some point around nine p.m., a trio of doctors approached us in the waiting room. From the grim looks on their faces, I knew the news couldn't be good. One of them spoke:

"We don't think Jackie is going to make it through the night."

If you are married, imagine what those words mean to you. If you have a child, brother, sister, mother, or father, fighting for his or her life, just imagine what those few words would do to your insides.

Gloria and I immediately got down on our knees and we prayed. But I couldn't help my mind from wandering. What had gone so terribly wrong? What had happened in the operating room that the routine removal of a placenta turned into a life-threatening situation? The only response from the doctors was that Jackie was hemorrhaging and losing blood very quickly. She had lost the ability for her blood to clot. One of the doctors, Nick Spirtos, had come in from Stanford University Hospital to work on Jackie after being called by Dr. Jurow. It was a little confusing at the time why the medical director of a women's cancer center was here to help my wife. It turned out Dr. Spirtos had vast experience working in the reproductive area. As Gloria and I kneeled on the hospital floor, Dr. Spirtos looked at Gloria and said, "We're not going to quit and we will work hard to let you have your daughter and him his wife."

Now, I'm not a preacher, though my brother Jimmy now is back in Mississippi, and I certainly would never tell someone *what* to believe in. But I am a man of faith and to me, there is a distinction between faith and religion. Faith is believing in a higher power, whatever form that may take, and using that belief to help guide you through life. When I was a teenager back in Crawford and we would go to church as a family every Sunday, it was more of a chore than an experience. But as I grew older, I began to develop my own sense of faith that I could follow outside of a Sunday church service.

Faith has helped me immensely in times of crisis and danger, but also in times of joy: When my children were born, when I caught a touchdown, when I moved on in *Dancing with the Stars*, I never forgot to acknowledge my faith inside, a belief in something so strong that it provides you with the strength to make it through the difficult times. I believe there is a higher being and I pray to God all the time and give glory unto Him when I am blessed with success. Before football games, I would pray by myself in the locker room to have a successful and safe game.

My faith and belief in a higher power never meant so much as when Gloria and I kneeled on the hospital room floor with Jackie's life hanging in the balance.

Over the course of the next four hours, my life was turned upside down. In the same moment that God had blessed me with a beautiful little girl, he also may have been taking my wife away from me. I walked down to the nursery to catch glimpses of Jada and then returned to the hell of the waiting room. Jada was so beautiful that for an instant, it took my mind away from Jackie. By this point in the night, some of my close friends had arrived at the hospital, including Shawn Rogers, my roommate in my first 49ers training camp and still a great friend, and good buddy Ray Charles Brown, who played high school football with me back in Mississippi. We weren't given many medical updates as the night wore on but we did know that blood for Jackie was being flown in from Sacramento. She ended up needing 250 units of blood products.

Just a little after midnight we saw a patient being wheeled slowly down the hall to a recovery room. There were bloody sheets around him or her, IV bottles, tubes in his or her arms and coming from his or her mouth, and a whole team of doctors and nurses walking alongside. We weren't sure it was Jackie. After a few minutes passed, a nurse did confirm that it was my wife but that we still couldn't visit her "for another twenty minutes." The wait was excruciating but at least she was still alive. When we were given the okay,

Gloria, Shawn, Ray, and I walked into her room. You could barely distinguish that it was Jackie. Gloria was the last to walk in and fell to her knees as she recognized Jackie's toes and fingers. My life's companion, the mother of my three children, was clinging to life in that hospital room. She was breathing through a respirator and fighting for every breath. Despite the surgery that Dr. Spirtos had performed on Jackie during the last five hours, Jackie was still not out of the woods. From midnight when we saw her until the wee hours of the next day, we gave thanks to all of those people who had contributed the blood products to the Red Cross that were now saving Jackie's life. The more Jackie fought during and after surgery, the harder the doctors and nurses fought to save her.

Gloria believed that prayer had saved her daughter during the night and, in the ensuing days, she made sure that all of Mississippi said prayers as well, calling everyone she knew and telling them to call everyone *they* knew to pray for Jackie. We didn't need money, we didn't need flowers, we didn't need insurance—we simply needed prayers.

The next few days were touch and go. Jackie was moved from Mills Hospital to Stanford University the day after her surgery, to be under the watchful eye of Dr. Spirtos and the Stanford ICU team. Just when things were starting to look up, Jackie's kidneys stopped working and back to the operating room she went. With the assistance of the respirator, she could breathe, and eventually the surgeons were able to stop the profuse bleeding, as her blood began to clot. A machine hooked up to her alerted nurses if and when her blood stopped clotting. Fortunately, through all of this, Jackie was unconscious.

Now, keep in mind that Jackie was moved to Stanford the day after Jada was born and our newborn didn't go with her. Jada was back at Mills Hospital. The doctors and nurses at Mills had promised me they would be her family while I took care of Jackie. But I knew that if Jada wasn't there when Jackie woke up, I'd be in big trouble. Three days after her birth, Shawn and I went and picked up my littlest daughter, brought her home, dressed her in the clothes that Jackie had laid out before going into labor, wrapped her well, and took her to visit her mother. From that day forward, we would lay Jada on Jackie's stomach, so the two could bond. Though my wife was unconscious, remarkably, when Jada was on her stomach, Jackie's vital signs became stable or elevated.

During those first few weeks, I never left the hospital, despite the pleas of family and medical professionals. They joked that if I didn't get some rest I'd end up in the hospital bed next to Jackie. But I just couldn't stand being away from my wife. Eventually, the hospital staff were kind enough to find me an empty room on the third floor where I could shower, change clothes, and grab a few hours of sleep every night. During the days, I would read books and magazines to her, stroke her hair or hold her hand. (She would later tell me she hated it when I stroked her hair—how she knew that when she was unconscious is still a mystery.) I even learned how to read the medical machines monitoring Jackie to alert the nurses if something was abnormal.

Thankfully, Gloria and our housekeeper were there to take care of Jaqui, Jerry Jr., and little Jada. Doctors called Gloria in the mornings and afternoons to give her updates and at dinnertime she would head over to the hospital. I was constantly on the phone with my family back in Mississippi, providing them with the latest updates.

Jackie remained in a comalike state for three weeks. On more than one occasion, some of the doctors wanted to throw in the towel and turn off the respirator for the love of my life. But that wasn't going to happen! Always there with her faith, Gloria, Dr. Spirtos, and I kept asking for "one more day." Just as she began to improve, Jackie became septic and once again underwent surgery, this time on her intestines.

When she finally did awaken, in early June, she had no idea where she was, what the date was, or what had gone wrong. Remember, the last thing she was awake for was the birth of Jada. Jackie was too weak to write and couldn't speak hooked up to the respirator, so we got a lettered board for her to point to the letters and spell out words she wanted to say. She cried as we answered her questions about what had happened.

The process of recovery was very slow. After Jackie had been awake for two weeks, the doctors huddled to determine if she should be weaned from the respirator to breathe on her own—after all, she had been on it for five weeks. Every doctor but Dr. Spirtos suggested she stay on it. But Dr. Spirtos knew better; he knew that she had fought for her life in surgery that first night and knew she could fight her way through this next stage. So with nurses and doctors on standby to perform a tracheotomy if needed, they cautiously removed the respirator. Throughout the procedure, I was right there with her, coaching her through it, giving her words of encouragement. It was a difficult and tense moment as she took shallow breaths, then deeper ones, and relearned how to breathe unassisted. It was a big moment in her recovery.

The people in the 49ers organization were great in their support of us and allowed me to skip June mini-camp to be by Jackie's side (though I did show up for one day) as well as the first week of training camp in July. Over the course of Jackie's hospitalization, many teammates and coaches came by to show their support, including

Steve Young, Joe Montana, Guy McIntyre, Tom Rathman, and my west coast father, Bill Walsh.

Jackie was allowed to go home from the hospital three weeks after her respirator was removed but not before we had another major scare. About six days before her targeted release date, Jackie suddenly didn't have feeling in her legs or feet. She was, for the moment, paralyzed. The doctors conducted test after test to try to determine what was going on but nobody seemed to have the answers. If blood had moved through her spinal cord, the paralysis would have been permanent, but thankfully, tests revealed that it hadn't. The best explanation doctors had was that there had been so much pressure on the pelvic area during the trauma and resulting surgeries that the sciatic nerves serving her lower limbs were damaged. But no one knew if my wife would ever walk again. To this day, she says she was so weak that it was like her whole body was paralyzed.

Still, the doctors released her after two months in the hospital, and of course it was a joyous day for all of us when she finally came home. But by no means was she out of the woods. She was still so weak that she couldn't even keep saliva in her mouth. Therapists would come to the house to work with her but she had no strength to do the smallest of movements. Weeks passed and her strength slowly returned. Finally, she was able to sit up. Feeling soon returned to her legs, but therapists had to teach her how to walk again. She needed ankle braces, crutches, and a cane to help her walk. It would be another two and a half years before Jackie was completely recovered.

We never would have made it through the ordeal without the love and support of friends and family. Jackie's mother was a saint, staying for a year to help with the rehabilitation and the kids. She left for two weeks at one point to tend to affairs back in Mississippi, but was right back on a plane to San Francisco. She wasn't going to leave until she knew that her baby would be okay. One of Jackie's cousins, who was in her first year of medical school at Georgetown, withdrew from school so she could move to California for a year to help care for her; one of Jackie's sisters stayed with us for four or five months to lend a hand; and her best friend left a great job to come out for a month and lost that job in the process. My family called almost daily to offer their support. Many people made sacrifices for our family and I will always be grateful.

LIFE WILL THROW UNEXPECTED things at you. It could be a family trip to the local state park interrupted by a rainstorm or a freezing cold day in Chicago for the NFC championship game. It could be as joyful as the unexpected pregnancy of your wife or as grave as the unexpected deadly illness she is afflicted with. There are moments we just can't plan for. Coaches in all sports, especially football, try to prepare for everything, but they simply can't. There are too many factors that go into a game, too many things one can't control.

When I did eventually make it back to football full-time in July, it was tough to concentrate at first. In a way, practicing with my teammates was a great escape from what was going on at home for mere moments, but then my thoughts would turn back once again to Jackie.

As Jackie continued to recover at home, I was angry. Angry at whom? At what? I was angry that something as beautiful as giving birth could lead to such dire circumstances. Women all over the world give birth every day and it is so commonplace that when something goes awry, it's critical. It is seldom reported how many women suffer complications from childbirth. Women *die* bringing a new life into this world. My anger soon turned to thankfulness, as Jackie had survived the worst.

You have to cherish every moment. You can't take anything for granted. My world had been on the verge of collapse. I was *this close* to losing the love of my life. It certainly put a lot of things into perspective for me. There were times I took my relationship with my father for granted, and that, sadly, sticks with me after his passing, two years ago. I took for granted the cherished moments with my children who are now growing up so fast. Football was my life up to that point; all of my energy went into the game and it took a tragedy for me to realize it.

In my first ten years in the NFL, our family never took a real vacation. Can you believe that? With the available time in the off season and with our blessed financial situation, we could have traveled the world. But there was never a true off season for me as I went right to work on my conditioning as soon as the season ended. My family sacrificed a lot for me. I did always try to make it to my kids' school plays, games, and important events, as even in season, I was home by five p.m. or so. Still, there were moments that I took for granted, thinking there would be time for me to spend with them when I stopped playing. I should have known better. But Jada's birth and Jackie's resulting emergency helped put the people in my life at the top of my list.

# The Other Side of the Bay

As Jackie recovered at home, the 1996 football season got under way. My production over the season decreased slightly compared to previous years, as Father Time began to creep up on me. When Jackie was healthy enough, she started coming to games again. I would carry her into and out of the car and put her in her wheelchair to watch. We finished 12–4 and earned a wild card berth into the playoffs. But after beating Philadelphia in the wild card game, we bowed out to Green Bay in the divisional round. It is very difficult as a wild card team to advance to the Super Bowl. Not only do you play all the games on the road, but you have to win three games just to get to the Big Dance. That's why I was surprised that the Pittsburgh Steelers made it all the way in 2006.

After the 1996 season, I signed a seven-year deal to remain with San Francisco, but I doubted even at the time that I'd still be playing with the 49ers in the last years of the contract, as I would be further on in age and the financial burdens on the team increased. My doubts would prove to be well-founded.

In 1997, Steve Mariucci took over for George Seifert—and my season ended prematurely. Playing on the road against Tampa Bay in our opener, I was caught behind the line of scrimmage by the Buccaneers' big defensive lineman Warren Sapp on a reverse play. Sapp grabbed the face guards on my helmet, which turned my head and put enormous pressure on my left knee, forcing it into an awkward position. I knew something was wrong but I thought I'd be okay. When I returned to San Francisco, I had an MRI done on the knee, which revealed a tear in two of my four ligaments; I was done for the season. But I suppose, in retrospect, it wasn't all bad. It gave me some time to work on my golf game, a passion I had picked up ten years earlier.

I knew that every time I stepped onto the football field there was a chance that I could get hurt. We football players jeopardize our bodies playing the game. But I thought what Warren did was wrong and uncalled for. The fact that he held onto my facemask instead of letting go makes me think it was intentional. As a veteran, you know when you're in the wrong, and Warren knew. There is a code in football that should be respected. It pissed me off. I didn't want, and *still* don't want, an apology. Ironically, Warren and I later played together in Oakland and while I never brought up the facemask incident to him, and he never approached me about it, it still upsets me.

I was determined to get back on the field in 1997, despite the doubts of doctors. After working hard rehabbing the knee, doctors gave me the go-ahead to try to practice in early December. The 49ers planned on honoring Joe Montana and retiring his number during a Monday night game against Denver in mid-December, and I badly wanted to make it back for that. Never should have done it. After snaring a touchdown pass from Steve Young, I landed in the end zone on my rehabbed left knee and, though I was wearing a brace, it wasn't strong enough to withstand the pressure and I broke a bone in the knee. Though I was eager to play that night, I never would have suited up had team doctors stressed the risks to the knee. I never realized the knee could break. To this day, I think the San Francisco organization was thinking with their wallets, not their heads, and liked the promotional and commercial implications of my return on that Monday night despite the risks to me.

THE OFF SEASON IN 1998 was spent rehabbing my knee—again. But in February, the mood was made even worse when a practical joke created an embarrassing situation for my family and me.

Law enforcement officials had been eyeing a massage parlor in nearby Mountain View, California, for years, after reports of prostitution on premises. Though we have trainers on the 49ers staff, my teammates, particularly Gary Plummer, suggested that the Mountain View place was great for deep tissue massages. So the day I just happened to try the massage parlor out, the police raided the spa and locked it down. I knew right away that my teammates had played a trick on me, knowing that the spa did more than give great massages and knowing what a strait-laced "nerd" I was. As you can imagine, it didn't look good. I had worked hard to maintain a healthy and honorable lifestyle, and suddenly, it all could have vanished.

What I learned soon after that incident is that people are going to believe what they want to believe and there's not much I can do about it. My entire life, I had tried to please others and make them feel comfortable, but as I matured, I learned that you can't please everyone. If my reputation took a hit because of the practical joke, there was nothing I could do about it. The next day as the media were having a field day with the story, I still dropped my kids off at school and went about my day in the Bay Area. Life went on and so did my training.

In 1998, I came back confident and healthy but the 49ers stars of yesteryear had moved on and Super Bowls were a thing of the past. There was a crop of great up-and-coming wide receivers in San Francisco, including J. J. Stokes and Terrell Owens. I could see the writing on the wall. My production level had decreased, my big money years were soon to kick, and San Francisco had very capable receivers to take my place. In 1998, we went 12–4 and lost to Atlanta in the divisional playoffs. In 1999, we went a dismal 4–12 and followed that up with a whopping 6–10 record in 2000.

As the 2000 season drew to a close, I knew my time with the 49ers was coming to an end. Bill Walsh, my mentor, and now the 49ers general manager, was making all personnel decisions at the time and even he knew that the 49ers couldn't keep me and my contract on board. I'm sure it was a tough situation for Bill. In my last home game, against the Chicago Bears, which would end up being my going away party, I figured head coach Steve Mariucci would call my number on many plays, as a present to me and the fans. Well, it started off like that, and I had seven quick catches. But then the ball stopped coming my way and Terrell Owens ended up with an NFL single-game record of twenty catches. I quickly realized what was happening. If I had kept catching passes and had a spectacular day, it would have been harder for the organization to let me go, as the fan and media pressure would have been too great. Remember, it's a business. With my salary of 2.5 million dollars in 2001, the organization decided that I just couldn't fit under the salary structure. I thought I could still contribute in a big way and that they could have found a way to make things work.

As the final whistle sounded, I was surrounded by the media and held a pseudo press conference right there on the field, which I think was encouraged by the 49ers. They wanted to rush me out of there. Only Jerry Jr. was by my side, as he usually came onto the field after games. It upset me. The 49ers could have just come to me and been honest, letting me know they wanted to go with younger guys or had to make a move because of the salary cap and then arranged for a more formal press conference. But instead, they slighted me and my family after the years I had given them. I did take a lap around the field at Candlestick Park and my teammates gave me a lift on their shoulders.

BECAUSE IT'S ALL ABOUT the money, there are very few true "teams" anymore, with Bill Belichick's New England Patriots coming the closest in recent years. I would have loved to play for Bill. I admire his demeanor, his coaching philosophy with the insistence on team, and the fact that players want to play for him, just as they wanted to play for Bill Walsh. But Belichick and the Patriots are a rarity these days.

NFL football, more than ever, is about making money for the team owners and for the players. Free agency, which was instituted to create some balance in the league, has worked in achieving that goal, as any given team in any given year can reach the Super Bowl through off-season free agent signings. But as teams court free agents, players will say anything to find the most lucrative home.

If they get a bigger offer somewhere else—they're gone. Even offensive linemen are making serious money! With no contracts truly guaranteed and the risk of injury so high (the average NFL career lasts just four years), players want to get the most money out of the league that they can. Some high profile players have become individual corporations with teams of agents, lawyers, publicists, marketers, and image consultants all working to maximize the opportunities. I was so focused as a player that I didn't even consider surrounding myself with a personal Team Rice. I recall the media making a big deal out of the fact that I had few endorsement deals, pointing out that my workouts precluded me from having the time and that my personality wasn't very outgoing.

But you know what? If I could do it all over again, you bet I would seek out every off-the-field opportunity, though not to the level that it would have distracted me from football. Marketing opportunities for football players are limited compared to those for star athletes in other sports in which their faces are not hidden by helmets. It was a mistake not to take advantage of the opportunities when I had them. I should have invested in car dealerships and had my agent more actively seek out product endorsements. I don't believe I ever would have sacrificed my training or performance for these off-the-field opportunities but I do now see how valuable they are.

There was one endorsement idea that I tried but that didn't work out so well. After my wife's brush with death in 1996, Jackie and I became quite close with the man we credit with saving her life, Dr. Nick Spirtos from Stanford University. Nick is a wonderful doctor and a great human being and we embarked on a lifelong friendship. We often aided one another in charitable and/or business pursuits—one of which tasted delicious.

In 2001, Nick and I talked about developing a healthy alternative to the candy that young children were eating. We did our research, and designed a new line of fat-free, vitamin-formulated gummy snacks, which we called Jerry Rice Playmakers. At the time, gummy bear candy was extremely popular and we wanted to provide a somewhat healthier alternative. The candies were all sports-themed and came in lime, lemon, cherry, orange, blueberry, and watermelon. Every package contained all of the recommended daily allowances of folate and vitamins A, D, C, E, B, and $B_{12}$. We teamed up with a businessman with experience in the production and distribution of candy, and we were off! We agreed to donate 2 percent of all proceeds from the sale of Playmakers to the Women's Cancer Center in the Bay Area.

The candies initially shipped to 2,100 Kmart stores around the country, but things fell apart very quickly. Despite my heavy promotional efforts, which included appearances in close to fifteen states in just seven days, the candy never made an impact. Much of that we blame on our partner, whom we'll call Mr. Candy Businessman, and whom, it turns out, we shouldn't have put so much trust in. Customers who heard about Playmakers went to local stores to buy them, but the stores were not stocked, despite orders. Our partner just wasn't getting the merchandise out. My pride took a hit and we lost a great deal of money but I certainly learned some valuable business lessons along the way, including knowing whom to trust.

BILL WALSH WAS—and still is—the ultimate 49er and that made it more difficult for me to leave the organization. In 2000, my days in San Francisco did come to an end—but they weren't finished in the Bay Area. At the time, the Oakland Raiders had a tenacious head coach, a young man named Jon Gruden, who used to be an assistant coach with the 49ers. When it became clear that I wouldn't be return-ing to San Francisco, Jon made overtures to my agent and they en-tered into serious talks. Other teams were interested but from the start it was clear Oakland was the front-runner as they needed a re-ceiver and I was already in the Bay Area. Playing for the hated rivals would be tough but it would keep me at home. Not only did Jon think I could still contribute on the field but he saw a chance to stick it to the 49ers, whom he had grown to loathe. When Gruden was an of-fensive assistant with the 49ers, he made copies, ran the film projec-tor, and did other low-level tasks, which left a bad taste in his mouth.

So after sixteen seasons in a 49ers uniform, I became a member of "The Dark Side" in early June of 2001. Now, when you think of the Oakland Raiders, you probably think of owner Al Davis and his trademark sunglasses or the fanatical and sometimes scary Raiders fans. I didn't know what to expect moving across the Bay: Would the team accept me, coming from the 49ers? Would the Oakland fans boo me because I had been a nemesis for so long?

I remember, right after my initial press conference, heading to the locker room to get ready for my first practice. I was so used to putting on a San Francisco uniform and I knew it would be very awkward to have on silver or black or any other colors. As I typi-cally did, I put on a brand new pair of socks and a slick new pair of pants, and said aloud that the silver and black was starting to look good on me, something new teammate Tim Brown, whose locker was next to mine, and a few other players heard. Tim laughed out loud. As I slowly put on each new pad and each new part of the uniform, I looked better and better.

Remember, ever since high school, I had thought that presenta-tion and style were everything. I've never understood how someone could dress sloppily and not care about how they look. Even during halftimes of games, I would put on a clean uniform! As the 49ers equipment staff learned, and the Oakland staff would soon learn, I am *very* particular about what I wear. They often laid out four or five pairs of socks and pants for me because they had to fit *just right*. I would wear regular socks, then cut off the bottoms of the uniform pair and pull the elastic to my knee. There was the wipe towel that I would wear around my waist, a towel my 49ers teammates called the "Sweet Towel" after Walter Payton.

The way I prepare and the way I look are the most important parts of my performance. It's part of having the right attitude. I never wore sweat suits to the stadium on game days because they were special days—I wore business dress. And before I stepped onto the field, I shined my helmet and tried on brand new shoes. Those little things helped me feel great. I'm not saying you have to wear expensive clothes, but wear clothes that fit the occasion and make you feel your most confident.

If I looked good, I played good and by the time I pulled the Raiders jersey over my head for the first time, I was ready to play. Many writers questioned whether the great Tim Brown and I could coexist on the same team, but I never had a problem sharing passes with Tim. Honestly, I was honored to be on the field with him. At that point in our careers, we had already established ourselves and I knew we would get along just fine, as Tim displayed grace and class and understood that the team was above all else.

I also knew that coach Jon Gruden believed in me and, after meeting Al Davis for the first time and speaking with him at length, I knew he too felt I could contribute. Now Al is a very intellectual guy and a very smart football man. He may come off as a curmudgeon to the media, but I think it's all part of his plan to take distractions off his players and coaches. During our first conversation, I got the sense that he was picking my brain, trying to figure out exactly what made me the player I was. He believed I could still play the game and help lead his beloved franchise back to the Super Bowl, where they hadn't been since 1994. I also got that sense from the players, who accepted me immediately, probably because of what I had already accomplished.

On that Oakland team in 2001 was notorious linebacker Bill Romanowski, but this Bill wasn't the eager rookie I knew with the 49ers. He was very laid back when he first entered the NFL, willing to be coached and always a quiet presence. But after Bill left the 49ers to go to Philadelphia and then on to Denver, he turned from Bill into "Romo." He began taking pills and supplements and it changed his physique and his psyche. When we reunited in Oakland, I didn't know this guy anymore. He literally scared me. His muscles had exploded, his eyes looked bigger, and his temper on the game field and in practice was uncontrollable. His quick fuse led him to strike a teammate, Marcus Williams, in practice, breaking Marcus's left eye socket. (At trial in 2005, I testified in court when Marcus sued Bill. I didn't witness the incident so I couldn't testify to that, but when prodded by a prosecutor, I did acknowledge that I didn't condone what Bill had done.)

As training camp and the season got under way, I noticed some big differences in how things were run across the Bay. In San Francisco, dating back to the Walsh era, there was a demand for discipline and fundamentals, on and off the field. The way we practiced, the manner in which we handled wins and losses, the techniques we used on the smallest of plays—everything was about detail to the 49ers organization. The Raiders took a slightly different approach and much of that, I believe, came from Al Davis. His motto of "Just win, baby!" held true. He and the coaching staff didn't care what you did off the field or how you practiced, as long as you won.

With the 49ers, everything was first class, primarily because owner Eddie DeBartolo insisted it be that way. He took everything a step above everyone else—how we flew to games, where we stayed, what we ate. Oakland wasn't quite that way. There were players in San Francisco content with being backups who easily could have started for other teams but they loved the organization and the environment. (Eddie would later get caught up in a bribery scandal in Louisiana and be forced to hand over the 49ers reins to his sister and her husband. I regret not speaking up on his behalf at the time, as I knew his character and his selflessness despite this mistake.)

It was difficult at first to learn a whole new offensive system and, occasionally, Coach Gruden and I clashed over plays and routes. The offense that Jon ran was quite complex and I had to learn a new terminology, which I struggled with early on, despite my efforts to adapt. He was crazy, and still is, but I love the man. His nickname of "Chucky" (named after the doll in the *Child's Play* movie franchise) is right on, as those facial expressions and intense glare are what you are going to get with Jon. He has a stare that can make a grown man quiver.

As I adjusted to a new team for the first time in over sixteen years, I also felt a burning desire to succeed. I always had that drive but now I had another motivation: proving my old employer wrong. When players talk about leaving teams behind and say simply it is "time to move on," that's BS. An athlete enjoys nothing more than showing up a team that gave up on him, and I felt the same way. The 49ers believed I was ready to be put out to pasture but I believed otherwise.

For much of my career, Joe Montana or Steve Young was behind center. Now, it was Rich Gannon's turn. We never quite had the chemistry that Joe and I had, but we managed to find our groove. Rich had an awkward sidearm throwing motion, which was hard to read, but somehow he got the football where he wanted it to go. He often joked with me that he enjoyed throwing to me because every time I made a catch or a touchdown, his name was going down in the record books.

It was unfair that Gannon lived and worked under media comparisons to the great 49ers quarterback. I for one never liked it when writers or fans compared me to other players or former greats. I set my own standards for excellence. I respected great receivers like Lynn Swann, Drew Pearson, and Steve Largent but I never wanted to be compared to them. I remember my first few years in the league standing on the sidelines watching Largent play. It's not often as an offensive player that you watch the opposing team play offense, as you're typically on the bench looking over diagrams or talking to coaches. But Largent had such heart, such determination, and I respected that. And I loved watching him. He wasn't big, he wasn't fast, but he ran great receiving routes and made the catches. He had football speed. I was honored when I broke Steve's touchdown reception record and I kept a picture of him on a Wheaties cereal box in my locker—but only out of respect and admiration. I never liked comparisons to him.

Now, with comparisons in mind, imagine being the son of a professional athlete. It could have been really hard for my son, Jerry Jr. Imagine the pressure on him to be great in athletics when the inevitable comparisons to me began. But that pressure has never come from me. He did play football his freshman year in high school and, who knows, maybe he'll stick with it. I don't tell him what to play or how to play, I only ask that he work hard at whatever he chooses to do. I take a step back when it comes to Jerry, and only provide encouragement or instruction when needed. For example, after a recent basketball tournament in the summer, I noticed that he seemed a bit winded during the games so I suggested a different cardio training routine to help him perform better.

IN MY LAST SEASON with San Francisco, I had seventy-five catches for 805 receiving yards and scored seven touchdowns. My first year with Oakland in 2001, I finished with eighty-three catches and 1,139 yards while scoring nine touchdowns. *Take that, San Francisco.* The team itself capped off a 10–6 season by winning the AFC West division title. (The 49ers went 12–4 and lost in the wild card game in the playoffs.) In the first round of the playoffs, we beat the New York Jets to advance to the AFC title game against the New England Patriots. But our season ended sourly with the infamous "tuck rule" game, as it became known. After it appeared Patriots quarterback Tom Brady had fumbled the ball during a snowstorm late in the game and we recovered, the officials watched replays and concluded that Brady was not trying to tuck the ball back into his grasp, but rather throwing it forward which made the play an incomplete pass, not a fumble. (I, of course, disagreed.) The Patriots ended up tying the game and winning in overtime.

As I watched the impact that instant replay had—or didn't have—during the Super Bowl between the Pittsburgh Steelers and Seattle Seahawks, I was reminded of the tuck rule game and the reasons why I was never a big fan of instant replay—especially in the regular season. All it does is slow down and disrupt the rhythm of the game. And sometimes the right calls, as in the tuck rule game, aren't even made. The outcome of games should rest on the field with the players, coaches, and referee decisions, and not on a slow-motion replay.

At the conclusion of the 2001 season, the Raiders made many off-season changes, including one involving Jon Gruden. It was widely reported that Jon and Al Davis were not seeing eye-to-eye and Gruden was, in a way, traded to the Tampa Bay Buccaneers, with the Raiders getting four draft picks and eight million dollars' compensation for letting him sign with Tampa Bay. Now, I never saw the two go at it, but I could tell that Jon didn't like Al's meddling. Al was always watching practice and sometimes even stepped in to coach a bit, pulling players aside to give them instruction. No coach, including Jon, likes that. So the parting was probably a good thing for Jon—but ultimately not for the Raiders.

Al promoted offensive coordinator Bill Callahan to replace Jon in early 2002. The offense didn't change much and I was even more productive than in 2001, as we finished with an 11–5 overall record to advance to the playoffs. Rich Gannon was even named NFL MVP—an honor well deserved. We beat the New York Jets to open the playoffs as we had in 2001 and then the Tennessee Titans in the title game to advance to the Super Bowl. The Raiders had brought me in to help get them to the big game, and I think I had done my part. We were set to play the Tampa Bay Buccaneers—coached by Jon Gruden and who had beaten the San Francisco 49ers in the NFC title game—in San Diego for the championship.

Having already played in, and won, three Super Bowls, I knew about the media hype and the party-driven atmosphere—but many of my teammates did not. As I mentioned previously, the distractions can easily cause a player to lose focus. After arriving in San Diego and witnessing the hoopla, I think some of our players were in awe of the festivities. We weren't prepared, we weren't ready, and we weren't focused, so when the opportunity came to speak up, I did, just as I had in 1995 with the 49ers after players missed curfew.

But even though I pleaded with the Raiders players about saving the partying for another time, about how the world was watching, I could tell by their body language that they weren't interested. Instead of looking at me as a guy sharing his experience, I think many of them saw me as an old man giving them a lecture. Times had changed. We all would pay the price.

My Raiders teammates and I suspect that sometime between the last practice before the Super Bowl and the Super Bowl itself, Bill Callahan and Rich Gannon made the joint decision that Rich would change his throwing process for the game—that he would try to throw off defenders by looking to one side of the field but throwing to the other. Neither Coach Callahan nor Rich talked to the wide receivers of a new strategy before the game, so we have no way of knowing if any conversations actually took place, but regardless, we were all thrown off. We weren't even given the chance to fight for the ball because, initially, we didn't know where it was going. But Buccaneers coach Jon Gruden knew Rich's game, having contributed tremendously to his development as a quarterback, and told safety John Lynch to instruct the secondary to hold back. "Stay home, stay home!" I remember Lynch yelling to the secondary. It was as if Gruden were standing next to Rich throughout the game, reading his thoughts.

The game was a disaster, to put it mildly. Despite the Bucs defense picking up on Rich's plan early, the score was tied 3–3 going into the second quarter. But the Bucs exploded for seventeen second-quarter points and we never got close again. They intercepted us five times and ran three of those back for touchdowns. How bad was our offense? On nine straight possessions, we had two first downs and never made it past Tampa Bay's forty-yard line.

Jon Gruden's Bucs were better prepared for the big game than we were—and I stress the *we* because we all lost as a team and I was part of the reason. I finished with only five catches for seventy-seven yards (though forty-eight of those yards came on a fourth quarter touchdown catch).

But I still think some of our offensive difficulties can be attributed to what we speculate was Rich and Coach Callahan changing the passing game without telling the receivers. And even after they realized Coach Gruden and the Bucs were reading our passes, they refused to make adjustments. At halftime, I expected Coach Callahan to go over an alternate strategy to attack the Bucs in the second half. After all, halftime gives a team the chance to re-evaluate its plan and make small adjustments to turn a game completely around. But we didn't do that. In fact, I don't think Coach Callahan had that perspective all season, and it cost us several regular-season games.

Having come from the 49ers, where we prided ourselves on being able to quickly assess our opponents' plan and evaluate our own mistakes early, I wasn't used to the frustration that comes with not using halftime to develop a different system of plays. I further wasn't used to having a quarterback who wouldn't adjust to the opposing team's defensive strategy, having played with Joe Montana and Steve Young. But when Rich gets a game plan he sticks with it and he'll live and die with it. He's just that type of quarterback.

But we had strong leaders in Tim Brown, Charlie Garner, and myself, and a team of players who were downright hungry, so we took it upon ourselves to make adjustments during the season, despite the fact that we generally disagreed with the playcalling. This determination got us to the big game.

Of course, I took the loss very hard. I always took losses hard. When I made it to the NFL, everyone around me learned to leave me alone, sometimes for days, after a loss. I didn't want to talk, eat, or do anything other than play the game over and over again in my head. So you can just imagine what I felt like after losing on the greatest stage in the world—a first for me. What happened after the Super Bowl loss still flows through my mind in slow motion. I remember talking to the media and getting dressed in the locker room. I remember my inner and outer silence on the team bus, as opposed to many of my teammates, who seemed to take the loss as just another regular season game. They were happy just to have made it to the Super Bowl, apparently. Just getting there was never enough for me.

Once we arrived back at the hotel, I immediately went up to my room and closed the door behind me. It was only then, sitting on the edge of the bed, replaying the game in my mind, that it really hit me that we had lost. Tears began to roll down my cheeks.

But then, unlike after previous losses (though never on this scale), some atypical thoughts began to run through my head. Maybe we were supposed to lose the game? Maybe this was a way for my career to go full circle, as I had won, and now lost, Super Bowls? Maybe life won't end because we lost a football game? I was always so driven to win that losing meant I had let the world down. But something clicked in that hotel room in 2003. It was as if a side of me woke up to tell me that being a professional meant being able to lose, learn, and move on. So despite my desire to just lie on the bed and cry, I composed myself and headed to the team party downstairs in the hotel. Everybody else was at the party and it was my obligation to go, so I did. But it didn't bring a smile to my face and didn't lessen the pain. That loss stays with me.

Coming off a Super Bowl year you might think we'd be pretty good again. Wrong: 2003 was a farce. There was infighting on the team, sloppy play on the field, and a complete lack of focus. That might explain how we won just four games (though it was comforting to know that the 49ers also slipped to 7–9). I had just two touchdowns the entire season, the lowest total I had ever had in the NFL outside of my two-game season in 1997. Our offense went from being the second-best in the NFL in 2002 to one of the bottom five the following season. Things were going downhill quickly for the Oakland franchise. And where I was concerned, they wanted me to be more of a mentor to the younger guys, not a playing contributor. I had no problems teaching young players but I still felt that I could be a presence on the field.

Bill Callahan left Oakland to become the head coach of the Nebraska Cornhuskers and Al Davis brought in Norv Turner to be the new head coach of the Raiders. Norv was never really head coach material and hadn't been successful in that role. He couldn't control players, and guys like Charles Woodson walked all over him. Woodson routinely showed up for practice and meetings when he felt like it, along with some teammates. Even as we were losing, there was no sense of urgency.

As for me, my number was getting called less and less and I was taken out of games more and more. In the off season, the Raiders had let Tim Brown go and I could sense that a youth movement was on its way. I wasn't ready to quit playing just yet and with things in decline in Oakland, I wanted out and let management know. The out came in the form of an early October 2004 trade to the Seattle Seahawks for a seventh-round draft pick—not exactly ego enhancing.

To NFL PLAYERS, there are some teams and cities you would love to play for and there are others you try to avoid. For the most part, those decisions are based on the lifestyle a city offers. For example, when the Raiders played in Los Angeles, everyone wanted to play for them, because who wouldn't want the beaches and beautiful people of Hollywood? Oakland was not exactly Hollywood. The New York Giants were popular because of the Big Apple, and in the 1990s Miami became a hot destination because of South Beach and the sexy atmosphere. Then there were places you wanted to avoid, like Buffalo and Green Bay, where there wasn't much going on. Arizona had become popular because of the golf courses, restaurants, and proximity to Las Vegas and Los Angeles. Seattle? It wasn't a top destination but the city was vibrant with great food and an eclectic music scene and I looked forward to playing there.

Seattle coach Mike Holmgren, winner of Super Bowls with the Green Bay Packers and my offensive coordinator with the 49ers from 1989 to 1991, told me that he needed me in Seattle to help them win football games. The Seahawks already had three quality receivers in Koren Robinson, Bobby Engram, and Darrell Jackson, but Mike told me I would be in the mix. He needed my skills, but also wanted me to help mentor the young guys. Whenever a team makes a trade midseason, they are looking for instant help, and I planned on providing it. After having played in San Francisco for so many seasons and then a three-year stint with Oakland, I was now in my twentieth season in the NFL and forty-two years of age. There were rumblings in the media and in football circles that it was time for me to hang it up, just as there had been when I left the 49ers for Oakland. Some believed I would tarnish my legacy by continuing to play while others thought *how sad* for Jerry Rice—he just doesn't know when to quit. But you have to create your own destiny. I wasn't going to let anybody but me decide when it was time to retire. If I still had the drive and could still contribute, I was going to keep playing.

———

Leaving my family behind in the Bay Area in 2004 was tough, but not nearly as tough as what my father faced. For many months, in fact years, my father, Joe, had been sick with diabetes. He was a stubborn, proud man and wouldn't listen to the doctors when they told him what foods and activities to avoid. They even told him repeatedly he would die if he didn't change. Over the previous months, whenever Dad got *really* sick, he would be hospitalized so the doctors could monitor what went into his body. Surprise . . . each time he got well very quickly. But soon after being released, he would rapidly fall back into his old bad habits. That's a pattern that lasted for months—don't listen to the doctors, get really sick, go the hospital, get better, get released, don't listen to the doctors . . .

I had stayed in close touch with my parents throughout his illness and did what I could to help from afar, but eventually I flew to Mississippi to see my dad. He had been in a hospital in Starkville but by the time I visited him, he had been moved up to Jackson for treatment. He gave me a huge smile as I walked into his hospital room. I sat beside him and pleaded with him to take better care of himself. I told him that the doctors knew what they were doing and that all of us—including me—needed him around. I've said my father could be very mean but he also had a gentle side, and that's what we needed now. Before leaving, I told him, "I love you," and gave him a hug. As I walked out of the hospital that fall day, I knew he'd be back home in a matter of days, and I hoped that he would finally agree to take care of himself.

It was close to two weeks later when I received a call on my cell phone while at the Seattle training facilities. Jackie was calling to tell me my father had died. You can imagine the shock. I had just seen my father; we talked, we laughed, he smiled at me. He was getting better and was going to go home. What happened? I thought my father would live forever.

Until you have a very close family member pass away, it is hard to understand the pain. There had been people whom I knew well pass away, but never one in my immediate family. He was here one minute, gone the next. It was especially tough on me when I flew home to Mississippi for the funeral and walked into my parents' house in Starkville. I was just waiting to hear his voice or see him walk into the room.

As my dad aged, he grew harder and more angry. That smile the last time I saw him was a rare soft moment. He never came out and told me he was proud of me but I could tell by the look on his face that he was. As tough as he was, we knew he loved us, even when he didn't show it.

As the 2004 football season moved on, I thought of my dad often, sometimes in the locker room, sometimes driving alone in my car. He would always sit and watch my games on television back home in Starkville, and he would eventually travel to watch me play in the Super Bowls. But now I couldn't call my dad anymore. I guess you never really recover from losing a parent. There are periods even today when I think about who he was, what he meant to me, how he raised me. I know he is in a better place right now and I know he is still watching.

HE WAS WATCHING ME in my brief stay in Seattle, where I saw minimal action in thirteen games, making twenty-five catches for 362 yards while scoring three touchdowns. We did make the play-offs at 9–7, losing to the St. Louis Rams in the wild card game. As the season ended, it was a difficult time for me. During the season, it was tough being away from my family, and the often wet weather in Seattle didn't agree with me. Did I really want to keep playing? Did any team want me? Tendonitis in my left heel was a continued bother and I just wasn't sure I could play another season.

But I told my agent, Jim Steiner, to try to find a team. As a joke, Jim sent out a fax to all the NFL teams letting them know that a future Hall of Famer was available. He meant it in jest but the media reported it as if we were desperate and almost begging for a team to show interest.

The Denver Broncos and coach Mike Shanahan decided to give me a shot. So in July 2005, I suited up in my fourth different uniform and participated in preseason camp. The Broncos were already stocked at the receiver position, and I knew I had an outside shot at being one of the top three receivers. Mike had told me from the start that he'd be honest with me and I respected that. In our preseason games, I had just four catches for twenty-four yards. (By the way, there is no way the exhibition season should be five games. We should play two, maybe three. The risk of getting hurt is too high and most players don't even play at 100 percent. But of course the NFL is about business, and the more preseason games, the more revenue for owners.)

I could never fully show the Broncos what I could do because of my heel. Mike decided to go with a young guy at the third spot and, while seated in his office, he told me I would be the team's fourth receiver. I knew it was time. I didn't want to start over anywhere else. I would have loved to formally retire as a San Francisco 49er, but there were league rules that would have made it costly to the team and I would have taken up a roster spot, even for a day. (In the spring of 2006, I began discussions with the 49ers about signing with them for a day and then retiring with them in the fall. In August 2006, I signed a one-day contract with the 49ers and then retired officially as a member of the organization. In November, the 49ers celebrated my career in front of the home fans.)

Most people, when they decide to retire, don't hold a formal press conference to announce that they are leaving the job that they love. I felt like I was prepared for that moment on September 5, 2005, and I rehearsed a written statement. But being out there in Denver, in front of family and the media, I started to reflect on the memories of a two-decade career. The players whom I had fought alongside; the coaches who had helped elevate my game; the road trips into hostile stadiums. The tears started to well up and, despite my insistence I wouldn't cry, I did. I knew I had made some sort of mark on the game but I still wasn't sure what it was.

Many columnists, talk radio hosts, and other media types had already begun to declare that I was the greatest receiver in the history of football. Simply the best. Though it's flattering to think that, I know it's not necessarily true. I may hold many receiving records but that doesn't make me the best. I may have won three Super Bowls but that doesn't make me the best. Was it my ability to get open? Catch touchdowns in the clutch? Block for my teammates? To this day, I have never believed I was the best receiver ever. There were so many greats that came before me, and there are some incredible talents still suiting up. If I ever did believe I was the best, then complacency would have set in.

Who is the best actor of all time? The greatest dancer of our generation? The best golfer or basketball player or hockey star? How about the best author or painter or singer? What does best even mean? The dictionary may describe best as being better than all others—an unequal among peers, if you will. But who decides that? How can you ever truly know who is the best at something? Take sports. You could say that Babe Ruth was the greatest baseball player ever or that Michael Jordan was the best basketball player that ever lived. But a friend could insist that Willie Mays and Bill Russell were the best. Looking at statistics may reveal who was the most accomplished in a certain area but there are no statistics for the best. For example, maybe Jordan scored so many points because he was a ball hog or because his team played great defense and forced turnovers, allowing Jordan to take more shots. No one can argue against Jordan being among the greatest, but merely looking at statistics doesn't always tell the whole story.

Despite never believing I was the best, I do believe that I helped leave the game of football in good shape, in terms of the caliber of play. As I said good-bye that day in Denver, however, I was concerned about the character of the new faces in the NFL. Would they carry themselves, on and off the field, the way they should? Would they work hard, in season and out, to get better at their game? Would we ever see true teams again, like those we had in the early years of the San Francisco dynasty?

Aside from family, football was all I ever knew. It was all I had ever done since I was fifteen years old. I lived it, breathed it, loved it—so much so that I forgot to take a look at the bigger picture.

What am I going to do now? I am sure it's a question millions of us have asked after retiring or leaving a career. What can I do to fill the void in my life? I tell you this: If I could do it all over again, I would have been more prepared for the next challenge. I would have explored more options while playing in the NFL and taken advantage of opportunities while I was playing, so when I did retire, I had something to fall back on.

Though I was dying inside up on the podium at my retirement

press conference, I was actually excited for the next challenge. I know, it seems contradictory, but the more scared I was the more excited I became for what came next. At forty-four years old, I still had a lot of life to live and I knew myself well enough to know that I wouldn't waste it. Little did I know that my next experience would require me to wear heels.

# Rat-A-Tat-Tat

ON ONE OF OUR off-season workout days back in 1986, our trainer, Raymond Ferris, brought some golf clubs and balls to the track in San Carlos. I jokingly tried to hit some golf balls, always thinking how easy it was. I couldn't do it. I literally couldn't hit a stationary white ball. Of course, I took it as a challenge. I immediately began to play as much as I could to try to master the game. But I soon learned that you can't master golf. All of us, including the PGA professionals, have good days and bad days. I had never watched much golf on television before I began to play, but the difficulty I had in learning the game gave me a new respect for the pros and the patience they need to raise their game. And in golf, if you perform poorly, you have no one else to blame but yourself.

When I was in the NFL, I'd play a round of golf every Tuesday, our off day. Sometimes, if we had a half day Friday, I'd get in a second round as well. And most days before, and sometimes after, meetings and practice, I'd just drive to a nearby driving range to hit balls. In the off seasons, I definitely found time for golf. In my last few years in the NFL, I was even invited to play in celebrity golf tournaments around the country. All told, I probably entered ten of them. They provided me with a chance to compete against others and to see how well I was really playing. I've played rounds with Michael Jordan, Mario Lemieux, and Oscar de la Hoya. One thing is clear when you play golf with former athletes—they are in it to win it.

Right after I retired, I played almost every day, but there *had* to be more to life than golf. At least I hoped so. I had seen so many former teammates and players simply suffocate without the game of football. Like my former 49ers teammate Charles Haley, who retired in 1996, un-retired in 1998, retired again in 1999, and has struggled since leaving the NFL, constantly watching the games on TV and insisting that he should still be out there because he's "better than them." Charles has done a bit of coaching with the Detroit Lions so maybe that's the best transition for him.

I watched NFL games on Sundays in the weeks after announcing my retirement as I tried to figure out what I wanted to do next. Watching the games was enjoyable, and I, too, still felt that I could play. In fact, I was hoping during those first few months that the Broncos would call and ask me back. I wouldn't have "un-retired" to play with any other team, but I would have suited up again for Denver if they needed the help.

It was about that time in October that my agent, Jim Steiner, received an intriguing phone call from producers in Los Angeles, wondering if I wanted to be a participant on a television program called *Pros vs. Joes* on SpikeTV, a cable network geared toward men.

The premise of the show was to take a handful of professional athletes and allow regular "Joes" to try to beat them in various competitions. On many occasions throughout my career, regular guys have challenged me in the streets or out at a field to run a race against them—and believe or not, I've sometimes taken up the challenge. I remember being with Jackie and Jaqui on a college visit to Jackson State back home in Mississippi when I was approached by a Jackson State football player who insisted that he could "shut me down." So right there, in a plaza in the heart of campus, I raced him in a forty-yard dash and he tried to stop me off a mock line of scrimmage. He failed in both cases. Why did I take him up on the challenge? Because I wanted him to know that years of hard work got me to where I was and that humility is a good lesson learned.

I certainly didn't have much on my calendar at that moment when the *Pros vs. Joes* producers called, and they were offering us very good compensation for just a little time. Figuring that I would be competing against the Joes in football, I knew no Joe would ever beat me, so I really had no concern about how I'd look. Since television was an area I had begun to think about just after retirement, I thought maybe this was a vehicle to start the next phase of my life. So Jim and I talked over the offer and I agreed to be a participant on the first show. The producers wanted me to be the leader, the "captain of the ship" for the first episode, leading former basketball player Dennis Rodman, quarterback Jim McMahon, baseball player Matt Williams, and wrestler Goldberg.

The taping of the football competition between the Pros and Joes was slated for some cold nights in early December in Los Angeles. The major competition had me running four different pass routes and catching balls thrown by Jim. Each of the Joes—Patrick Alston, Tom Courtad, and Josh Lenn—would take turns trying to cover me. Right before we started to tape, I found out that there was tackling involved. This wouldn't be me in a warm-up suit jogging patterns. This would be helmets and full pads, head to toe. Even if the Joes couldn't stop the catch, they could tackle me before I reached the end zone and therefore earn the victory. When I learned there was tackling, I thought twice about the potential embarrassment and knew I had to up my game. *Okay, here we go,* I told myself. Especially considering that many of my former football peers would be watching, there was no way I was going to let any of the Joes stop me. And they didn't. One after another, I made the catches on great throws by Jim and scored touchdowns. It was easy for me.

Some of the staff of *Pros vs. Joes* suggested that I let one of the Joes catch me and tackle me, just to let one of them win. I wasn't going to let that happen. So I talked to Jim, and he agreed to take something off his throws so that the Joes could make the play, giving them a small victory.

When I signed up for the show, I didn't know the competition would be so serious and I certainly didn't know the producers would make this my show. As part of my contract, I was sent to New York City to do a lot of media promotion, and Karl Malone, who appeared on a different episode, was supposed to join me—but he was a no-show. So I was out there as the face, and spokesman, for *Pros vs. Joes* and the perception was that this was my show—but it wasn't.

Would I do the show again? Probably not. Especially if I knew what was coming later. I also should have done enough research to know that on SpikeTV, things can get a little nasty with craziness and foul language, because that's apparently what sells. But that isn't who I am. Still, on the positive side, the show gave me a glimpse into the world of television, and gave me some exposure to key decision makers in Hollywood.

THE FIRST SEASON of the ABC television show *Dancing with the Stars* was the surprise of the 2005 summer television season, luring in viewers of all ages, many of whom were not dancing fans. They tuned in to see how celebrities like actor John O'Hurley and former *Bachelorette* Trista Sutter fared at dancing. The reality television craze had been around for five years with shows like *Survivor, The Apprentice,* and *American Idol,* so *Dancing with the Stars* hit at the right time. I have to admit, I had only seen a few minutes of one of season one's episodes, accidentally tuning in while flipping the channels. It was dancing, for crying out loud! I had danced a bit as a kid and at weddings and parties, but not the kind of formal ballroom-type dancing they did on the show, so when Jim Steiner called me one day in the beginning of November to ask me if I was interested in competing on season two, I immediately replied, "No, are you crazy?"

But Jim wasn't about to give up that easily, since he knew how successful the first season had been and he thought this might be a great way for me to transition into major television work. He suggested that we research it a bit and think about it before getting back to the producers. Dancing in front of millions of people? What if I embarrassed myself? I had a reputation to think about! I knew nothing about dancing. There were a million reasons why I shouldn't do it, I told myself, but there was one thing that ultimately convinced me to try it: the challenge, of course. And I had never shied away from difficult tasks in the past. Yes, my image was important to me but since when did I let others dictate what I would do with my life? Especially at that point in my life, I knew that I had to take risks and get out of my comfort zone.

When I called Jim to tell him I would do it, I honestly thought I would be on the show for a few weeks before being eliminated. I mean, with no dance training, I was a bit awkward and figured I would be voted off the show in the first few rounds. Jackie and the girls were supportive of my decision but Jerry Jr. was worried about my reputation—and his. He was apprehensive about his macho, football-playing dad donning dance shoes. What would his friends think? (As the weeks went on, Jerry—and his friends—became some of my biggest dancing fans!)

The producers of the show and ABC also compensated me very well for appearing, I have to admit, and that money was up-front—it didn't matter if I was eliminated the first week or the last week.

For those of you unfamiliar with *Dancing with the Stars*, the premise of the show is this: Pairs of dancers, comprised of a professional dancer and a celebrity, compete on a weekly basis to be crowned champion. One couple is voted off the show every week, until just one is left standing. Like *American Idol*, there are three judges who give critiques after each dance and who, like Simon Cowell, are brutally honest. Ultimately, the judges and the American public decide who stays and who goes through phone-in and online voting, combined with the judges' own scores. Every week, before the actual competition, each pair would practice on their own, with all of their work captured by camera crews.

For season two, the dance pairings were: Louis van Amstel (dancer) and Lisa Rinna (host/soap star); Edyta Sliwinska (dancer) and George Hamilton (actor); Jonathan Roberts (dancer) and Giselle Fernandez (television anchor); Ashly Del Grosso (dancer) and Master P (rapper); Max Chmerkovsky (dancer) and Tia Carrere (actress); Andrea Hale (dancer) and Kenny Mayne (sportscaster); Nick Kosovich (dancer) and Tatum O'Neal (actress); Tony Dovolani (dancer) and Stacy Keibler (professional wrestler); Cheryl Burke (dancer) and Drew Lachey (musician). Oh, and then there was Anna Trebunskaya and Jerry Rice.

Anna was originally from Russia but now lived near my family outside of San Jose, California. She was a professional dancer by trade, teaming up with contestant (and husband) Jonathan Roberts to compete in dance competitions around the world. Anna's parents owned a dance studio in Russia and were professional ballroom dancers themselves, so it was fitting that she began to compete in Russia at seven years of age, before moving to America with her parents when she was seventeen. Her specialty? Latin dance, for which she has won numerous awards. This was my partner. As you can imagine, I was the tiniest bit intimidated before our first practice session.

With camera crews filming, I drove to the Starlite Dance Hall in Sunnyvale, California, about thirty minutes from our home, to meet Anna for the first time. She knew very little about me, other than the biographical information she had been given, and was certainly no fan of the NFL. (But it turns out her husband was a huge 49ers fan and knew all about me.) After we exchanged introductions and started to talk, Anna asked me what I wanted out of the competition. With gut instinct, I told her I wanted to win. I was quite serious about doing my best and trying to beat out the other couples and I got the sense that Anna saw this in my facial expressions.

The premiere episode of *Dancing with the Stars* was to be taped January 5 in Los Angeles and our first practice took place a little over a month beforehand, right after the Thanksgiving holiday. The Latin cha-cha was our first dance, and we got right to work.

The cha-cha is a fun, upbeat dance, originally from Cuba, with tricky steps choreographed to the beat. As Anna demonstrated the routine and moves to me, I wanted to run. There was just no way I would be able to dance the cha-cha. I just wanted to say sorry, and bolt for the door. But I had agreed to try it, and of course I would. Then Anna gave me a pair of dancing shoes with heels on them, as Latin dances require a lot of pressure on the balls of your feet. Not only would I dance in front of millions, but I had to do it in heels!

Slowly, I began to learn the steps, but I had two left feet, as they say. Now, for a man, and for a professional football player, I thought I had good feet. That is, after all of those years running receiving routes I knew how to explode off my feet and how to dance on the field. When quarterbacks threw the ball to the sidelines and I had to catch the ball while touching both feet in bounds, it was like I was dancing. I called it the Rat-A-Tat-Tat. But dancing on a football field was far easier than this. Though I was frustrated during our first four-hour session and a bit embarrassed, I knew I had to get over it. I had to let go of who I was on the football field and start from scratch.

I TOOK A RISK when I chose to attend small Division I-AA Mississippi Valley State. I took a risk asking out Jackie in that gymnasium in 1984. I took a risk in asking her to marry me. I took risks in NFL contract negotiations. I took physical risks every Sunday. I took risks leaving San Francisco for Oakland, and in venturing on to Seattle and Denver. I took a risk with Jerry Rice Playmakers. I took a risk doing *Pros vs. Joes*. And I certainly took a risk with *Dancing with the Stars*. Taking a risk means you are putting something on the line—your security or comfort zone, your reputation, your life—but it also means you have something wonderful to gain.

I don't regret any of the chances I've taken in life. If there is one common theme among the thousands of comments I get from fans around the country these days, it's that it meant something to them that I was willing to put myself out there for *Dancing with the Stars*—that I risked embarrassing myself and my reputation to try something so unlike me. It would have been *comfortable* for me to just keep playing golf every day but then I wouldn't have been experiencing life. I come across so many people in all walks of life who have the urge to try something new, but simply can't pull the trigger to do it. Maybe they are scared of failing or maybe they don't want to risk what they have. The biggest reason I find people don't take risks is that, well, they're comfortable where they are. That may make you feel safe but it won't allow you to grow.

You know who took a lot of risks in his life? My father. I know it sounds strange, considering the picture I've painted here of a hard, strong man, but he took a risk the way he lived. How he ate bad foods and the toll that his work took on him is just a start. My father always provided for us but he also liked to spend his money on vices. He burned the candle at both ends. He looked at life as some crazy thing to get through so you might as well live every day as if it is your last.

I was thinking of the risks that I had taken in my life as I drove home after the first session in Sunnyvale, wondering what I had gotten myself into. I was doubtful I could pull this off, but, as I had learned from events in my life, these doubts keep me honest and humble.

Over the next few weeks, we practiced and practiced and practiced, usually four hours a day at the Sunnyvale studio or at the Imperial Dance Studio in Redwood City. There was always a *Dancing with the Stars* camera crew taping our every move—and misstep. Anna was a great teacher and coach those first few weeks and she was very patient with me. I respected how hard she worked and was aware that her experience could teach me a lot. First, she had to learn the routine herself; then instruct me on the steps; then build it into the routine; then put that routine to music, making sure the count and steps were on beat. In ballroom dancing, the man is supposed to lead, but we were a long way from that. At home at night, I would practice the steps over and over again, usually with our youngest daughter, nine-year-old Jada, who loved to dance. She would even give me instructions at home like, "Dad, you have to move your hips more!"

So each day those first few weeks, Anna and I practiced in the dance studio for hours, not counting the time we spent practicing on our own off camera. Remember that camera crews were with us recording everything, and I was always conscious of them. I knew that if I stumbled or fell on my face they would show it to all of America. I also had to restrain myself when I wanted to let out a curse word when I was frustrated. With just a handful of days left before the first live television performance in Los Angeles, the routine was up to a minute and a half—a full routine. I really felt uncomfortable and didn't know how to count the music. I felt like a rookie with the 49ers again.

We then went to Los Angeles for the show, beginning a routine we would follow for the next eight weeks. We flew down on Wednesday morning and had a scheduled slot to practice on the stage, block the dance for the cameras, and rehearse to the music on CD. On that initial trip, I had the chance to meet some of my competitors, who were at the television studio for the same purpose. I immediately clicked with George Hamilton, who had a flair for entertaining; Stacy Keibler was kind and energetic; Drew Lachey was down-to-earth and funny.

But to be honest, I was a bit dismayed to learn that Stacy had taken ballet classes for sixteen years and that Drew, as a member of 98 Degrees, had learned dance moves from top choreographers. I thought it was totally unfair for them to compete against complete novices like myself and I don't think the producers should have let them participate. We were at a disadvantage. I mean, I thought the whole point of *Dancing with the Stars* was to watch celebrities with no dance experience tackle ballroom dancing.

After every couple had the chance to practice on Wednesday, we were left to our own devices that evening. Jackie had flown down to help calm my nerves. I was a wreck. After practicing in the studio early in the day, it hit me just how big this was going to be: a band, the audience, judges, not to mention the millions watching at home.

The three judges were Bruno Tonioli from Britain, who would be honest but choose his words carefully; Carrie Ann Inaba, a choreographer who "tells it like it is," regardless of how the criticism makes you feel; and Len Goodman, the kind, wise man of the show with great one-liners. On Thursday morning, we had to check in by eleven a.m., and all of the pairs used the next few hours practicing and perfecting. On each Thursday, the producers did a mock show at about three thirty p.m., a full dress rehearsal. The real audience and judges were there as well. That first mock show was an out-of-body experience for me. After Anna and I finished our trial run, I thought we did okay—not great.

After we finished the dance and listened to the judges' comments, we retreated backstage to a large greenroom, where we were interviewed by cohost Samantha Harris and where the competitors all mingled. Even during the mock show, I wanted to impress everyone. (It was clear early on that Drew and Stacy could dance.)

There wasn't much time before the live east coast taping at five p.m. of *Dancing with the Stars,* and I used the time to redo wardrobe and get makeup touch-ups. Moments before the show went on, I felt a rush of anticipation. I know what you're thinking—that I'd performed in front of much larger crowds than the one in the studio. True, I've played football in front of seventy thousand fans but I had a helmet on to hide my emotions, and I knew what I was doing on the football field. Having on a full uniform had always sheltered me from what I perceived were critical eyes judging me; now I felt totally exposed.

When it was our turn, we took the floor and I quickly spotted Jackie in the audience right before we began. She was seated in the front row. I was so conscious of counting the steps that I completely ignored the audience during the dance, which I would later learn was a mistake. With so much concentration on the mechanics, I looked, well, mechanical and stiff. I was relieved that I hadn't fallen on my face but I also knew our performance wasn't great. The judges' comments were not positive.

We immediately left the stage. We were interviewed backstage as our scores were announced. We received twenty-one out of a possible thirty from the judges, but those scores still had to be combined with the millions of voters after the show. There was another area off the greenroom, which I referred to as the vent room. It was the chance for the producers to catch your raw emotions and thoughts (something made popular in many MTV reality series), and all the contestants vented after they danced.

After every couple had performed, they brought us all back out onto the stage for the conclusion of the first show. I was thankful it was over.

As you might expect, my cell phone was overwhelmed with messages from family and friends, some of whom had had no idea that I was even participating in *Dancing with the Stars*. The messages were positive and encouraging, though some buddies got in a few cracks at my expense. Thursday evening we were on our own as we awaited the results show Friday afternoon. Every Friday morning during the show season, I tried to get out and golf on a local Los Angeles course to keep up my game and to keep my mind off the results. Just as we had on Thursdays, on Fridays we had to rehearse the elimination show, which made for some fun speculation. The mock show included the judges, who gave us their comments, and all of us were trying to decipher what their facial expressions and words meant. We were looking for any clue as to who would be eliminated. It was pretty clear that it would not be Drew Lachey or Stacy Keibler, who did a tremendous job their first time out on Thursday night. As for me, I knew I was a better dancer than George Hamilton, Master P, and Kenny Mayne, but who knew what America would think?

We survived and moved on to week two. Sportscaster Kenny Mayne was the first to go. I was excited but knew I had to get a lot better. Anna and I returned to the Bay Area on Friday night and agreed to meet at two p.m. on Saturday to start an entirely different routine.

There were things over the ensuing weeks that perhaps the viewing public never truly understood. For example, on Thursdays when the show was taped, every couple was stressed out and still learning and tinkering with their dance routines, right up until showtime. There was also the soreness and stiffness associated with using muscles many of us were using for the first time and, of course, there were the always-present camera crews taping every word and action.

So on Saturday morning, January 7, Anna and I were back in the dance studio, this time working on the quickstep. Remember that Anna had to first learn all of the routines before she even began to teach me, so she was working twice as hard. In the ensuing days, when I would do my thing around San Francisco—dropping the kids off at school, visiting the gym, grabbing a latte at a local Starbucks—I was amazed at how many people stopped me to say, "Nice job" or to wish me good luck. Some of my kids' friends at school would tell me how surprised they were that I could dance. Despite my initial shortcomings as a dancer, I noticed that I somehow was able to inspire members of the viewing audience. People who never followed the NFL were suddenly new fans of mine.

Over the next four weeks, Anna and I continued to work hard and kept advancing in the competition. We scored a twenty-three in week two with the quickstep but a nineteen in week three with a jive, after which Len Goodman commented, "Jerry Rice? It was more like geriatric." We were lucky to move on that week. As the weeks passed, I became more comfortable on the dance floor and less mechanical. I even took a ballet class arranged by Anna, as she thought it would help me to be light on my toes for the foxtrot in week four. The lesson seemed to pay off, and the judges were impressed. I hit my stride with the samba in week five, when I was so relaxed that I could actually be playful on the dance floor, engaging audience members during routines and just having a good time. I had watched others like George Hamilton who, though he wasn't the greatest dancer, brought entertainment to his routines through his facial expressions. I picked up on his traits and soon found myself making hand gestures, winking at the judges or cracking a smile midroutine. I was able to show the true me, and it also showed the judges and America that I wasn't focused on my steps and on counting beats.

Former teammates would call me to lend their support. On separate occasions I ran into Joe Montana and Steve Young, who both told me I was doing a great job. Still, I am sure there were people who wanted me to fail for whatever reason, just as when I played in the NFL. And just as I did while playing football, I picked up the newspapers to read what "they" were saying about my dancing and my decision to participate. *Why would the great Jerry Rice do this to his legacy?* Some of the criticism was harsh, but I simply took it as further motivation. I wanted to prove them all wrong, and make them look stupid in the process, the same approach I took with the judges.

My mother tells me she and many of our family and friends would gather around the television sets back home in Mississippi to watch each episode of *Dancing with the Stars.* She would call me often during the season to give me little hints on my moves. And Gloria would host parties and encourage all of her family and friends to vote.

Anna and I had a good relationship. She was very demanding and insisted on being the best—sound familiar? There were times in rehearsals when we almost boiled to the argument point, but we always just took a timeout or moved on to something else. She was also very honest. If we did a routine in rehearsal or on the show that she felt we could have done much better, she told me as much. All through the experience, I kept reminding myself how difficult it must be for a professional dancer like Anna to have the patience to deal with a novice like me.

By the middle of February, after week seven, Anna and I had advanced to the final three pairings for the grand finale. Drew Lachey and his partner, Cheryl Burke, were the favorites to win it all and Stacy and her partner, Tony Dovolani, were a close second. Some fans were surprised that Anna and I were even still around, believing that Lisa Rinna and her partner were better than Anna and me. But I think America liked the fact that I stayed humble and worked hard over the season to improve. At least I could tell that impressed the three judges. By that point in the competition, I had secretly begun to think we could win the whole thing. There's a difference between believing you *can* win and believing you *will* win. The former is having some confidence, the latter is having all the confidence. For her part, Anna told me to forget about winning it all and just to focus on working hard.

By February, our workdays in the dance studios had doubled from four hours a day to eight hours a day. Dance was now what I did.

The momentum and buzz surrounding the finale was incredible. This was my new Super Bowl. During the season, *Dancing with the Stars* regularly pulled in the biggest audience, eclipsing the monster *Survivor* in total viewers!

When it came time for the final show, I was amazingly relaxed. The producers decided that the finale would be a two-hour show Thursday night followed by a two-hour show the following Sunday—like the NFL, anything to score additional ad revenue.

The additional time of course meant additional dances for us, which meant a hectic final week. In the finale, each couple would do three routines: one, the exact dance we had performed in prior weeks; two, a dance of our choosing; and three, a variation of a previous dance. Anna and I chose the foxtrot and the previously dreaded cha-cha. America could vote only after the Thursday show and the judges' vote would be split between the two nights.

I remember right before our first dance, I was playing with

the audience and even blew Jackie a kiss. Anna and I did the fox-trot, which we felt was one of our best routines, and the one in which I really began to break out of my shell in week four. We both thought we had performed well. For our second dance, which was a freestyle choice left up to each couple, Anna chose the Kool and the Gang song "Celebration" from 1980. In prac-tice, Anna had suggested we go all the way with the dance, which included wearing seventies attire—me wearing a huge Afro wig. My first reaction was, "No way!" But ultimately, I agreed that the costumes would show a different side to us and maybe give us an edge. Winning was in my brain. No one had any idea we would be dressed up, not even the judges, as we wore regular dance attire in the dress rehearsal and saved the costumes for the live performance.

When the cameras rolled, we hammed it up with the judges and audience while wearing wigs and bell-bottom pants. We had a blast. Drew and Stacy danced confidently, too, but despite their prowess no one—including us—knew what to expect when the re-sults were announced on Sunday night's finale.

On the Sunday night show, all three couples performed one last dance before one couple was eliminated. Between Thursday and Sunday's show, we stayed in Los Angeles and Anna and I practiced, practiced, practiced. We had one more shot to win the whole thing and we would cha-cha—our very shaky first dance from week one. I was a bit nervous but the "wow factor" had taken over. I was in the finals of *Dancing with the Stars*!

To the surprise of many—but not to me—Stacy and Tony were sent home first. Though Stacy had the background in dance, it just seemed the American public wasn't behind her. There was cer-tainly shock in the audience, and later, among critics, when I bested Stacy for a spot in the final two. After Stacy was eliminated, there was still time to fill, so the producers showed packaged stories and presented some more dances on stage. Before the hosts announced the overall winner, I honestly thought Anna and I would win.

But we didn't.

Drew and Cheryl were crowned the champions. I admit finishing second stunk, especially after all we had put into the show. It was like losing in the Super Bowl; a horrible feeling with nothing gained from second place. I was hurt, sad, and believed that we'd deserved to win the competition. The improvement I showed over the course of the competition and the fact that I—not Drew—was a true dance novice should have given us the crown, as that's what I thought the show was all about. Even judge Bruno Tonioli called Anna and me "the Lady and the Champ." The finale was watched by an average of 27.1 million viewers, crushing the number that watched the closing ceremonies of the Olympic Games in Torino, Italy.

So how did I manage to end up in the last two, anyway? Though the judges were tough on me from the very start, the voters seemed to support me as the weeks went on. As I would soon learn, they connected with my struggle to master dancing. They envisioned themselves trying to learn the intricate steps and I think that helped me. I was one of them.

As a professional football player, I imagine I impressed people with the touchdown catches and Super Bowl wins. But did I inspire anybody? I hope so. You see, it's one thing for a child or an adult to watch a game on television or in person and be in awe of a professional athlete; it's a completely different thing for them to be moved enough to take action. I would rather have a young fan want to emulate my work ethic than want to be the next Jerry Rice. It's not the end result that inspires people, it's the journey. It's not records or wealth or titles, it's how you get all of those things that people connect with. That's why I take so much joy when *Dancing with the Stars* fans tell me how I inspired them to try new things, even ballroom dancing.

When I look back on the *Dancing with the Stars* experience, I have no regrets. Millions of Americans got a chance to see a totally different side of me. I think I surprised a lot of people who didn't know I had a playful, softer side and for many, it was the first time they saw me without a helmet. Even former teammates whom I played alongside for years commented that they never knew I was like this.

Competing on *Dancing with the Stars* was the perfect choice for me. It provided me with a new challenge that took my mind away from the only thing I had ever known. I couldn't think about football and mope on Sundays because I was focused on *DWS*. It made my transition from football player to media personality seamless. The show opened up so many doors for me in the next stage of my life. For example, as the popularity of the show rose in late January, organizers of the Miss America Pageant called and invited me to be a judge for the 2006 competition. The next thing I knew I was on an all-expenses-paid trip to Las Vegas and sitting next to fellow judge Brian McKnight judging the women, eventually helping to crown Jennifer Berry the new Miss America. It was a memorable experience.

*Dancing with the Stars* also opened up to me the world of television entertainment. I had done thousands of interviews before, but they were all related to my football career. Now, I was appearing on shows like *Jimmy Kimmel Live, Entertainment Tonight, Good Morn-*

*ing America,* and many others. Since the show ended in the spring of 2006, I've met with many producers about a variety of roles, from hosting reality shows to acting in movies. Twenty years ago I was way too shy to even think about a job on television but now, it's what I want to do.

# Epilogue

So, BACK TO THE question, what's next for me? I don't know, I really don't know, but I am excited about the opportunities that lie ahead. My guess would be more television work in the entertainment and sports worlds, a few movie roles, some golf tournaments (of course!). I had the chance to play a round of golf with Donald Trump in July and he offered me free membership to all the Trump courses around the world—not bad.

Jackie and I were recently flipping through old picture albums, wondering where the time has gone. We looked at pictures of Jaqui from almost twenty years ago when we would bring her to a nearby Benihana restaurant and rest her on the table while we ate. The staff still remembers her to this day. Jaqui went off to Georgetown University in 2005 and I missed her terribly. But now she has decided to take a year off from Georgetown to pursue her real passion: singing. She had seen a television special on pop star Beyoncé Knowles, who described how she just knew she wanted to sing and whose parents arranged for vocal coaches and did everything they could to make her dream come true. Jaqui wanted to do the same. When she first approached me about taking time off from Georgetown, I was of course hesitant, concerned about her leaving her education. But my support swung in her direction when she pointed out to me that I had followed my dream of playing football. I didn't want her to have any regrets looking back. As of this writing, Jaqui is deep into her new career and we are hoping she will continue her college education out here on the west coast.

Jerry Jr. is coming into his own as a young man, currently a sophomore in high school. He loves basketball, and I love watching him practice and play, and spent much of last summer on the road with his traveling youth team. Little Jada is my baby, now ten and doing all the things that ten-year-old girls do. Unlike my father, who got harder as the years passed by, I have become more soft, especially toward my children. I tell them I love them every chance I get.

In August 2006, I was inducted into the College Football Hall of Fame at South Bend—a natural location for the Hall since South Bend, Indiana, is the home of the University of Notre Dame (a legendary football school in addition to being a top academic institution). It was an honor to join the ranks of college football's elite, including my former teammates and Notre Dame alumni Joe Montana and Tim Brown.

The celebration opened with a parade where I was able to get up close and personally greet fans and shake their hands—I much prefer the opportunity to be interactive than simply sit in a car and wave. And it was amazing how even in this football town people used our brief meetings to say, "You were great on *Dancing with the Stars!*" I still can't get over how many people connected to that show, but I admit, the compliments are always flattering.

But the day was dedicated to football, and my fellow inductees wouldn't let me forget it. During an afternoon sandlot game, they wouldn't turn me loose! I've been retired for a year and I'm *still* getting double-teamed! The informal game did put me in the right frame of mind for the last part of the day's festivities which was working with kids on basic football skills in a sort of mini training camp. It was a busy but fun day. I just loved being in that environment.

As for the NFL, it goes on without me. Despite all the Pro Bowls and the NFL records that I set, I wouldn't say that I revolutionized the wide receiver position in football, but I would admit that I, along with guys like Michael Irvin and Cris Carter and Tim Brown, changed what coaches and general managers look for in a receiver. Cris was a possession receiver, a player who made spectacular catches all over the field. Michael was, simply, a playmaker. He could make a routine five-yard catch and turn it into a touchdown. Tim made the receiver's position look easy. I think I was a combination of all of them. I think all of us in the late 1980s and early 1990s made receiving a critical position in an offense which required speed, height, and an ability to make big plays—and that's the prototypical wide receiver today.

When I look around the NFL in 2006 at the new generation of receivers, I see some remarkable talent, but not all of it put to good use. If Randy Moss had the drive to be great, he could be the greatest wide receiver to ever play the game—he's that good. His size and speed and ability to get open make him virtually untouchable. But Randy is more of a follower than a leader, and plays up to his abilities only when he wants to, and those two characteristics will prevent him from ever reaching his potential. Cincinnati's Chad Johnson is a very good player but a showman like Deion and T.O. He likes to run his mouth and he keeps a list of defensive backs he has burned and talks about upcoming opponents he will toast. (Bill Walsh told me never to say or do anything to give an opponent extra motivation.) Chad is, however, honest, and when he does have a bad game, he gives credit to the defenders. He is a showman, and I wouldn't be surprised if he gained a bigger share of the spotlight in coming years. The Indianapolis Colts' Marvin Harrison is the little guy with a lot of heart. He plays with respect for himself and his teammates and I like how he handles himself. He doesn't do things to bring attention to himself, he just plays the game.

As for T.O., I played with Terrell Owens in San Francisco and attempted to impart whatever wisdom I could give to him in our years together. When I left San Francisco for Oakland, the torch was passed to Terrell. In fact, in my farewell game against Chicago when Terrell had the twenty catches for an NFL record, I gave him the game ball, as he clearly was the star. Today, he is the best player in the NFL. No one can play him one-on-one and his six-foot-three, 225-pound frame is imposing. His problem, like so many other good players, is the attitude. As I mentioned earlier, I wonder how much better he could be if he just stuck to football, not entertainment. If you cross Terrell, he can't ever seem to let it go. I watched from afar the soap opera that was the Philadelphia Eagles in 2005, and couldn't believe what I heard and read. After having a huge game the previous Super Bowl while playing hurt, Terrell had Philly in his palm—but he wanted more. His conduct and comments about coaches and teammates eventually found him on the inactive list for the season. Public battles like that never would have happened back in my day, when the veterans would have squashed things from the start. Terrell and quarterback Donovan McNabb acted like children the way they went back and forth taking shots at each other.

Speaking of Donovan, he throws the ball well and, especially in previous years, he added a dimension with his quick feet, somehow eluding defenders to make plays. He is a very good quarterback. But when he had his chance on the biggest stage—the Super Bowl—he wilted. There is no tomorrow when it comes to the Super Bowl and great players play their best in the biggest games. He didn't. He made bad decisions and it cost his team.

Peyton Manning, like Donovan, is a consistently good quarterback during the regular season and his offense has put up some gaudy numbers in past seasons. But has Peyton won a very big game? Until he does, I won't consider him a great quarterback. People never thought Steve Young was a great QB until he won the big game, and I think fans and the media have the same feelings toward Peyton. New England quarterback Tom Brady is often said to be the next Joe Montana. Maybe, but not now. He does work hard and some of his mannerisms (such as his calmness) are the same as Joe's, but he shouldn't be compared to him just yet. I wonder how Tom would do without a great team behind him.

Ben Roethlisberger led the Pittsburgh Steelers to a Super Bowl title at a very young age, which is quite impressive, but his reckless behavior off the field may cost him a shot at greatness. In the summer of 2006, he crashed his motorcycle while not wearing a helmet and it almost cost him his life. He plays with that same edge and I don't think he is going to change. (I used to drive a Harley-Davidson motorcycle for fun until one day I took it onto the freeway. I was scared out of my mind and felt so vulnerable and exposed that I stopped riding motorcycles.) The reigning NFL MVP, Shaun Alexander from Seattle, is widely considered to be one of the best to play running back. But I can't put him up there with the best. A lot of his teammates don't feel he is of the highest caliber and do not believe he is a leader—a characteristic that all the greats have.

The next generation of NFL stars is upon us. I followed the 2006 NFL draft, and had the opportunity to watch a lot of the top draft picks play during the season. Tops on my list is New Orleans Saints' Reggie Bush, who reminds me a lot of Gale Sayers. He can explode on a moment's notice and stop on a dime. Reggie appears to be very mature and knows what he needs to do, and he'll be a star. Next up is Tennessee Titans' rookie quarterback Vince Young, who may have an awkward throwing motion, but he gets the ball where it needs to go and his big frame and quick feet make him a weapon. As for former USC quarterback and now Arizona Cardinals' signal caller Matt Leinart, he is a winner, that's for sure, but his arm strength is not the best. Is he *that* good or was he simply surrounded by great talent at USC? I think the talent around him made him appear better than he is, and we will wait to see how effective he can be in the NFL.

As for the San Francisco 49ers, I don't see a bright future the way things are going now. I don't know much about head coach Mike Nolan but I know that the players on the roster are merely okay. Young quarterback Alex Smith is overrated and is not the next great 49ers QB. Offensive coordinator Norv Turner has never really proven himself to be a very good coach. And John York, the current owner, is more interested in marketing and promotional opportunities than he is in bringing top-flight players to San Francisco.

———

MY TWENTY-PLUS YEARS playing in the NFL and the television opportunities that have come up after my career have left Jackie and me in great financial shape, and we are blessed with a bright future. But I've never forgotten what my life was like before I got drafted, when I picked cotton and corn just to help my family eat. My parents taught my siblings and me that money won't fix many of the problems that a little love and understanding can cure. Money won't bring you happiness. Yes, you can buy material things, but so what? Are you happy? I like to think that if I had become a schoolteacher or a mechanic and made less money than I did playing football, I'd still have the same philosophy.

All you have to do is look at our three children and how they approach money. When people get to know our family, they are routinely impressed that our kids are not spoiled. They don't always wear the fanciest articles of clothing or drive the hottest cars or spend money like it is an unlimited resource. We've taught Jaqui, Jerry Jr., and Jada to value money and to know that there are a lot more important things in life than the mighty dollar.

I know that Jackie and I will continue to be involved in charities, donating our time and money to worthwhile causes. In the spring of 2006, I lent my name and time to the Arthritis Foundation and did media interviews around the country, to help raise awareness of that debilitating disease. Sixty-six million Americans suffer from some form of arthritis, which costs the U.S. economy tens of billions annually. With multiple surgeries on my knees during my playing days, a few of my joints have minor arthritis in them but I hope *I* don't become a casualty of the disease. As I work with the foundation, I hear so many moving stories from arthritis sufferers, from a middle-aged man who wanted to be able to play with his son to a mom who just wanted to climb her son's high school bleachers to watch him play football.

We will do a lot more traveling as a family now, making up for so many missed trips early in my career, and we will continue to return annually to Mississippi, where it all began for us.

My biggest role now is as a father. And I'm still learning. I used to think I was pretty flexible when playing in the NFL, constantly changing the way I played to accommodate new quarterbacks or coaches. But nothing can compare to the flexibility it takes to be a parent.

Sometimes you need to be stern and tough while other times a hug and a kiss are in order. As a parent, I've certainly made my share of mistakes. Maybe I have punished one of my children too harshly or maybe been too easy. Maybe whipping them like my father did to me was not the best way to teach them. Maybe I neglected them at times when I should have been there. I know I am not alone as a parent questioning my parenting skills and decisions. I do know that as I have gotten older, I make more flexible choices as an adult and parent, and think things through a bit more, including how I deal with my children. Being flexible means you have the maturity and experience to be accommodating. It means sticking to your core values but being willing to allow others theirs. Being flexible is about accepting criticism and not being complacent.

I am going to keep working hard at every new challenge and seek out opportunities that I never thought possible. *Dancing with the Stars* opened my eyes to a world full of exciting adventures and I plan to take them all. I'm now a host of a football show on Sirius Satellite Radio three times a week and continue to look for new television hosting opportunities. I'm doing more corporate speaking, sharing what I've learned with people from all walks of life. I still love to golf and try to play three or four times a week. I still work out almost every day, doing short and long sprints on the track and hitting the gym to lift weights afterward, though I haven't run the dreaded two-and-a-half-mile hill in San Carlos in quite some time. It is important that all of us keep exercising as we age not only for our physical health but also for our mental well-being. I wonder if my father would still be here if he took care of his body.

As I age, I also cherish more the relationships that I had with some of my teammates from long ago. A few months back, I showed up at Joe Montana's book signing at a local store and stood in line like everyone else just to get his autograph. When I got to the front, as Joe looked down to sign, I asked him to personalize it. He realized it was me. His shock was masked by laughter. There are still times when I can be hard on others, especially if I sense they are disloyal or not being straight with me. I can also be hard on my kids, as I insist that they treat others—and one another—with respect. But for the most part, I'm just laid-back Jerry.

I am now forty-four years old and just starting to understand what life is all about. What our journeys mean. For me, the fear of failure, the doubts, the struggle, is who I am, for better or for worse. I know that my childhood shaped me, and I've acknowledged that. But I also wonder if I ever would have had the success that I've enjoyed without those voices in my head telling me I couldn't fail or wouldn't succeed. As my children grow older and as I move on to the next stage of my life, I've learned to manage the voices. Maximizing my inner drive first meant understanding that my drive was a fear of failure and then learning how to use it.

No one else lives your life but you, so you might as well take hold of it and make it your own. Think about who you are and where you want to go, and then go there. We are all in charge of our own destinies, whatever they may be. Whether your destiny is in fashion design or catering, retail management or teaching, follow your dreams no matter what. Along the way in your journey, there will be those who will want to disrupt your path; they will want to shape your destiny for you. They may be family and friends who doubt you or a jealous coworker who doesn't want you to succeed, but you have to be able to put the negativity aside. Why should someone else get to choose your path? You can control what you accomplish. Are you willing to sacrifice to get there? Are you going to take the initiative and make it happen? Let me tell you that the world won't wait for you and you can't wait for other people to get your life going. Go for it!

I really think *Dancing with the Stars* changed my life and my outlook. I really started living a few months ago when the show finished up. This is my life and I am going to live it to the fullest and enjoy every moment. I am going to continue to try new things, even when others tell me not to. I am going to put myself and my reputation on the line seeking out my passions. I am very fortunate that the first phase of my life provided me with the means to seek out challenges in the second phase. I will have successes and I will have failures, but I won't go down without fighting for every scrap of life. I am committed to my life. Life is short. So commit yourself to making the most out of the time that you have.

And if you see me in the gym or on a golf course or at the grocery store, please come over and introduce yourself, and if reading my journey has inspired you at all—even just a little—then let me know. That's the most gratifying thing to me.

# ACKNOWLEDGMENTS

From Jerry Rice

Finding the right words to thank the many people in my life who have contributed to my journey has proved to be difficult. A simple thank-you seems insufficient, and the list of those who have helped me over the years is too long to include here. As for this book, the list is shorter, but nonetheless important.

A big thank-you to my coauthor, Brian Curtis, who helped guide me in putting my thoughts into words, and with whom I spent a great deal of time talking about life—and golf. Brian is the consummate professional and a man I now consider a friend.

To the editors and staff at the Random House Publishing Group, especially Adam Korn and Bruce Tracy, who embraced my vision from the start and who believed in me along the way, Gina

Centrello, the Random House Publishing Group president and publisher, and Libby McGuire, Ballantine publisher, for giving me the chance. Cindy Murray is a wonderful publicist, and Brian McLendon's input on publicity was critical. Porscha Burke was a big fan of the project from early on.

Jillian Manus, my literary agent and California neighbor, helped make the idea of this book a reality and provided me with experienced advice to make it happen. My longtime agent, Jim Steiner, has been a rock throughout my football career and introduced me to the world of ballroom dancing through *Dancing with the Stars*. Lon Rosen at William Morris has opened up the world of television to me.

With all of my projects and commitments, I couldn't make it without the help of my trusted assistant, Sasha Marin Taylor, who was instrumental in helping Brian and me complete this book.

Thanks to my mother and late father, whose love made me into the man I am today, and to my mother-in-law, Gloria, for helping out in more ways than I can count.

To the people who mean the most to me—Jackie, Jaqui, Jerry Jr., and Jada—words cannot express the gratitude that I owe to all of you, for your understanding all these years and for putting up with my passions and my drive. Our lives are just beginning.


## From Brian Curtis

It has been a pleasure helping Jerry capture his inner thoughts, and I admire not only his work ethic, but also his enormous heart and good sense of humor. Between phone calls on his way to the gym to ride-alongs in a golf cart, I learned what makes Jerry tick, and I hope we have revealed that to you.

Thanks to Adam and Bruce and everyone at the Random House Publishing Group for your invaluable advice and editing. A thank-you as well to our research assistant, Steve Brauntuch. To my agent, Janet Pawson, for guiding me and keeping me sane.

To my parents and extended family, I hope your journeys have been fulfilling.

To my loving wife and my beautiful daughter my thanks for letting me type away and for understanding when the phone rang and I said, "It's Jerry." I love you both.

## About the Authors

JERRY RICE attended Mississippi Valley State University and was selected by the San Francisco 49ers in the first round of the 1985 draft. In his twenty-year football career, he was elected Rookie of the Year (1985), was selected to the Pro Bowl thirteen times, won three Super Bowl rings (and was named the MVP of Super Bowl XXIII), and was chosen for the NFL's 75th Anniversary and All-Time teams. Now a broadcast personality and commentator, he lives in California with his wife and their three children.

BRIAN CURTIS is the author of *Every Week a Season* and *The Men of March* and the coauthor, with Nick Saban, of *How Good Do You Want to Be?* A former reporter for FOX Sports Net, he is the host of *Taking Issue* on CBS Sports' College Sports Television and a football and basketball reporter for the network. He lives in New York with his wife and daughter.

## About the Type

This book was set in Caslon, a typeface first designed in 1722 by William Caslon. Its widespread use by most English printers in the early eighteenth century soon supplanted the Dutch typefaces that had formerly prevailed. The roman is considered a "workhorse" typeface due to its pleasant, open appearance, while the italic is exceedingly decorative.